POWER, HOLINESS, *and* EVANGELISM

Rediscovering God's Purity, Power, and Passion for the Lost

POWER, HOLINESS, and EVANGELISM

Rediscovering God's Purity, Power, and Passion for the Lost

Contributing Authors

Steve Beard • Pablo Bottari • Harvey R. Brown, Jr.
Michael L. Brown • Randy Clark • Pablo Deiros
Gordon D. Fee • Chris Heuertz • Scott McDermott
Carlos Mraida • Mark Nysewander
Stephen A. Seamands

Compiled by **Randy Clark**

Destiny Image® Publishers, Inc.
P.O. Box 310
Shippensburg, PA 17257-0310

"Speaking to the Purposes of God for This Generation
and for the Generations to Come"

ISBN 1-56043-345-0
Library of Congress Catalog Card Number: 99-74409

For Worldwide Distribution
Printed in the U.S.A.

Second Printing: 1999   Third Printing: 2000

This book and all other Destiny Image, Revival Press, Mercy Place, Fresh Bread, and Treasure House books are available at Christian bookstores and distributors worldwide.

For a U.S. bookstore nearest you, call **1-800-722-6774**.
For more information on foreign distributors, call **717-532-3040**.
Or reach us on the Internet: **http://www.reapernet.com**

Dedication

I dedicate this book to my wife DeAnne, who has been such a help to me in ministry. I love her heart's desire for experiencing the power of God, to walk in His holiness, and to reach the lost. I want to thank her and honor her for her passionate prayers for the spiritual well-being of our children and for her sacrifice of love in managing our home while I am away so much of the time. "This is dedicated to the one I love."

Acknowledgments

I want to express my thanks to Steve Beard, who helped me in so many different ways to bring this book into reality. From encouraging me to write it, when I first shared the idea for the book, to helping me secure the various authors; from editing my chapter from its original length to a more reasonable one, to all the many other ways you have helped me; I thank you, Steve, for believing in me and in this book.

I also want to thank my Publisher, Don Nori, and Acquisitions Editor, Don Milam, for their encouragement and support during the writing process. Thank you for your commitment to and heart for revival. Thank you for your words of encouragement, your emotional support, and your prayer support.

I thank Elizabeth Allen, my Staff Publisher at Destiny Image, for your excitement over the book. I hope it affects others the way it has you!

I want to thank Gail Cornell-Smith, my personal assistant, for her support in this and all other projects. I also want to thank Sue Stevens for proofing my chapter for me, as well as all the other ways she has been a help to me.

A special thanks to Hendrickson Publishers for allowing me to use Chapter 11 from Gordon Fee's *Paul, the Spirit, and the People of God*. This is a great book, and I encourage all the readers to read it.

Finally, I want to thank all the other authors of this book. Thanks to Steve Beard, Pablo Bottari, Dr. Harvey R. Brown, Jr., Dr. Michael L. Brown, Dr. Pablo Deiros, Dr. Gordon D. Fee, Chris Heuertz, Dr. Scott McDermott, Dr. Carlos Mraida, Mark Nysewander, and Dr. Stephen A. Seamands.

Endorsements

"This book represents a courageous step forward in spiritual and theological cross-fertilization. It brings together crucial elements of Christian witness and experience that for too long have been isolated from each other. It opens up a conversation that is sorely needed in the contemporary Church. All who yearn for the presence of the Kingdom here and now will be both inspired and challenged by its proposals and arguments. They will find here a vision that seeks to be open to all that God has given us in the gospel and in the Church."

—William J. Abraham
The Albert Cook Outler Professor of Wesley Studies
Perkins School of Theology
Southern Methodist University

"Caution: The fire in this book may leap off the pages on to the reader. God's fire empowers, purifies, and emboldens our witness. This is the way the Church is supposed to be. Highly recommended."

—Dr. Bill Bright
Founder, President
Campus Crusade for Christ International

"This book is about holistic Pentecostalism. It is a Pentecostalism that is finding power to evangelize through repentance and holiness. It is a movement that is discovering expressions of the Holy Spirit in compassion for the poor and in crusades for social justice. It is a Pentecostalism that embraces a doctrine of the Kingdom of God that promises both personal and social regeneration."

—Tony Campolo, Ph.D.
Professor of Sociology
Eastern College
St. Davids, Pennsylvania

"This is an excellent collaboration, to keep our eyes focused in the right places as we pray and prepare for revival. It contains excellent material. *Power, Holiness, and Evangelism* will provide substance for your faith, insight into key areas of developing maturity, and hope for the future. The writers are sensible, biblical, and passionate, and they care for the lost. So if you can identify with all of that, this book is for you!"

—Gerald Coates
Pioneer Network
Speaker, Author, Broadcaster

"*Power, Holiness, and Evangelism* are present truth words that every believer and every church leader should fully understand. The writers who partnered together have certainly given definition, depth, scope, and purpose to their powerful words. A great equipping book for all who hear what the Spirit is saying today."

—Pastor Frank Damazio
City Bible Church (formerly Bible Temple)
Portland, Oregon

"Randy Clark has brilliantly highlighted in this symposium the values that God has been emphasizing and recovering in order to lead His Church into the third millennium and beyond to our Lord's return. The Holy Spirit, world harvest, holiness and healing, the good news to the poor, prophecy, and the theology of power and the theology of politics—these are things that, together with many thousands, I personally wish to live and die for, for Jesus!"

—Roger Forster
Founder of Ichthus Christian Fellowship
Co-founder of March for Jesus

"The brilliance of this book is its reuniting of that which never was meant to be separated—purity and power. To have purity without power is like having a spectacular locomotive and train on a sure track...but, unfortunately, with no power to move forward. To have power without purity is like having a coal-stoked locomotive, moving forward under a full head of steam, but spinning its wheels in mud because there are no railroad tracks. To have purity and power is to have a locomotive (power) running toward its destination on firmly built tracks (purity). This book profoundly affirms Jesus' merger of 'spirit'—anointing and power—and 'truth'—integrity and purity (see Jn. 4:24). Thanks to these writers, the 'great divorce' of purity and power has ended in a grand remarriage!"

—Dr. Jim Garlow
Senior Pastor, Skyline Wesleyan Church
San Diego, California

"Randy Clark has tapped into one of the most important messages on the heart of God for this generation. I have read a number of books on the subject of purity and holiness, but this is one of the meatiest and most powerful of them all."

—Cindy Jacobs
Co-Founder, Generals of Intercession

"This timely book, in which Randy Clark has brought together able people with different perspectives and backgrounds, demonstrates that the time is long overdue for the remarriage not only of the Word and Spirit but also of purity and power. It recounts thrilling experiences of what God has been doing in recent times. This has whet my own appetite to see this more and more—and not just in the Third World but in all our churches on both sides of the Atlantic."

—R.T. Kendall
Westminster Chapel
London, England

"This fine book is a most welcome call to holiness arising out of the current renewal. These messages and testimonies bring the themes of power and purity together for the sake of effective mission. The book lifts up the foundational truth that the people of God are meant to be a demonstration of God's existence and proof positive of the Kingdom of God breaking into the world."

—Dr. Clark Pinnock
Professor, Theologian, Author
McMaster Divinity College

"Fresh winds of the Spirit are flowing throughout the world. This book is what I call 'neo-charismatic.' It documents and teaches a healthy expression of a dynamic movement. Those who want to understand the contemporary scene in the Church and world need to read *Power, Holiness, and Evangelism*. A frequent criticism of the 'Holy Spirit people' is that they have lost their moral compass. This book combines an emphasis on purity of heart and life (sanctification) and the empowerment of the Holy Spirit for witness and service. I recommend *Power, Holiness, and Evangelism: Rediscovering God's Purity, Power, and Passion for the Lost* to all who are interested in new manifestations of the faith and world revival."

—Dr. Ed Robb
Author, Church Reformer, United Methodist Evangelist

"This is an imperfect book, written in an imprecise style, by an improbable collection of authors. But is has a single aim, a passionate tone, and some very valuable biblical insights. So I recommend it to all who long to see purity of heart and power in ministry once again joined in our lives and movements. I believe only this 'unity of the Spirit' will produce the risking evangelism necessary to reach our lost and hurting world."

—Dr. David A. Seamands
Author of *Healing for Damaged Emotions*

"We should have known this—how could we have not? Our power over the enemy is directly related to our purity and interwoven with effective evangelism. When such a group of credentialed ministries march en masse toward you, correctively stating and restating with firm tact and divine diplomacy these facts, one can't help but listen. And listen we must! The future of the Church is at stake and this book has some answers. These authors speak eloquently, confirming what you have felt, affirming what you intuitively knew. It's time to 'clean up' so we can 'mop up'!"

—Tommy Tenney
Author, Revivalist

Contents

Foreword
Introduction

Foreword

I first met Randy Clark at a "Catch the Fire Rally" at Founders Inn in Virginia Beach in 1994. I was invited to talk to an overflow audience about the spiritual manifestations that occurred in most of the great revivals of the past. A few months later, I spoke at another rally in St. Louis where Randy and I had several conversations about historic revivals and the central place of holiness teaching and experience in many of them. Although we came from very different backgrounds, we both felt that a major need at this time was a new emphasis on answering the biblical call to holiness as part of the present-day moving of the Spirit around the world.

Since I was born in a church that was both "Pentecostal" and "Holiness" (the Pentecostal Holiness Church), my own roots were deeply planted in the Holiness tradition. As a young man, I felt called to research the connection between Methodism, the classical Holiness movement, the Pentecostal movement, and the Charismatic movement. After years of research leading to a Ph.D. degree, my findings convinced me that the common root of all these major moves of God was a deep yearning for personal holiness that drove thousands of seekers to the "mourners bench" to seek a "second blessing" of sanctification, which at times was also called a "baptism in the Holy Spirit."

In the early days of the Pentecostal Revival, under Charles Parham in Topeka and William J. Seymour at Azusa Street, the holiness experience was as highly prized as the charismatic experiences of speaking in tongues and exercising other spiritual gifts. The Azusa Street testimony was, "Praise God, I am saved, sanctified, and filled with the Holy Ghost." In those days, seekers often experienced titanic spiritual struggles in their quest to be free from the power of sin. Indeed, I am now convinced that many times the experience of "sanctification" was in reality a "deliverance" from demonic powers.

As a matter of fact, the Pentecostal movement was birthed in the Holiness movement with most of the first leaders, including Parham and Seymour, coming from Wesleyan-Holiness backgrounds. One of the tragedies of the time was the divisions within the Holiness churches over the question of tongues and other of the *charismata*, which led to tragic divisions and separations. Stephen A. Seamands calls this "the great divorce" that should never have taken place.

In later years the sanctification experience was de-emphasized within Pentecostalism as thousands of people entered the movement from non-Wesleyan backgrounds. Yet, a strong emphasis on personal holiness continued to permeate the movement until the years after World War II.

As revival again sweeps around the world, there seems to be a heart cry for freedom from the sin and corruption that spews forth from the media and occasionally destroys the ministries of some of the most famous Christian leaders in the land. In an age of "cheap grace" where anything goes from both the pulpit and the pew, there has come a "stomach turning point" among many Christians who refuse to be carried along with the moral confusion and "wickedness in high places" that is so prevalent today.

Many of the personal stories in this book read very much like the testimonies of the old "Shouting Methodists" and the Holiness folk caught up in the fiery camp meetings of previous generations. Perhaps the pendulum is swinging back toward the radical holiness that changed the lives of millions and brought on the Pentecostal Revival. If so, it would be some of the best news I have heard in decades.

As a young man, I was deeply influenced by the British Pentecostal theologian, Noel Brooks, who once managed the healing crusades of George Jeffries. In his day, he saw many moral shipwrecks of pastors and evangelists who spoke in tongues but continued to live disgraceful and immoral lives. As a result, in 1959 he wrote a classic book entitled *Pardon, Purity, and Power: The Threefold Ministry of the Holy Spirit*. These "threefold ministries" referred to justification (*pardon*), sanctification (*purity*), and baptism in the Holy Spirit (*power*). He pointed out that these three have always been joined together from the days of the New Testament down to modern times. Mark Rutland makes the same point when he calls the union "a holy wedlock." If any one of the three was missing, the Church began to lose its power. In other words, "what God has joined together, let no man put asunder."

Randy Clark's book, *Power, Holiness, and Evangelism*, makes much the same point for a new generation of readers. It is indeed a timely book with a crucial message for the modern Church. Holiness is not an option; it is a necessity if we are to see the Lord. As these chapters make clear, in the debates about the relative importance of purity and power, it is not "either/or," but "both/and." If this century can end with an army of millions of sanctified pastors, evangelists, teachers, prophets, and apostles marching forward in the power and gifts of the Holy Spirit, then the final goal of evangelizing the world will be within the reach of this generation. Amen! So be it!

Vinson Synan
Regent University
Virginia Beach, Virginia

Introduction

A Vision

My vision for this book is that it will light fires among God's people. I pray that it will create in us a great, burning desire for lives that are filled with joy, growing in personal holiness, free from the enemy's clever bondages, and effective in evangelism. There is a great need for greater evangelism to be demonstrated by the lives of believers, but it must not be limited merely to seeking intellectual acceptance of one's set of beliefs. Ultimately we need an evangelism that also includes a living demonstration of God's power to set His people free.

I hope that this book will create a vision among the diverse groups within God's Church—a vision of a transformed Church, clean and powerful, drawing in the greatest harvest of all time. We need a vision of a Church made up of transformed believers who are filled with the Spirit, obedient to His leading, and who may properly be called "disciples." We need a Church filled with believers who have put aside all bondages and "besetting sins" and who are living victorious lives. We need a Church made of believers who know that they are not their own, that they have been bought with a price, that they belong to another—the Lord Jesus Christ—and who are making new *disciples* of all new believers!

Additionally, I pray that this book will help build bridges among churches and denominations from various theological streams that have historically been tragically divided.

Only a Dream?

Is it realistic to even dream of a Church that is characterized by unity, power-filled lives, and personal holiness? I believe so. After all, it was not long ago when it seemed totally unrealistic to talk about the falling of the Iron Curtain. Nevertheless, it did fall. In these remarkable days we live in, I believe that God is creating a new hunger for holiness, for world missions, and for evangelism of the lost billions.

In my opinion, the contributors to this book demonstrate that these goals are achievable. All have seen their churches experience a renewed emphasis on seeking personal holiness, God's power, and the salvation of lost souls. All believe that God is also giving us both the will and the power to live holy, consecrated lives and to evangelize as part of our lifestyles. All agree that God is calling us to evangelize our world as He is setting us free.

These contributing authors are also bridge builders. They come from the United Methodist, Assemblies of God, post-denominational Charismatic, Vineyard, and Baptist churches. They come from churches with long traditions—the oldest Baptist church in Argentina and the second oldest Baptist church in Latin America—and from movements that are relatively new, such as the Vineyard, as well as from young independent churches. Not incidentally, they also have impressive credentials: Seven of them have earned their doctorates and at least half that many presently teach at seminaries, Bible colleges, or Bible schools.

I hope that this is not just a dream. There is much to do. More people are living now and will die within this generation than have lived in all previous human history.

A Problem

One of our most immediate problems in realizing this dream is that the Church as we know it is not transformed; it is not clean and powerful; and it is not victorious. It is not full of healed, delivered, self-denying, transformed believers. Rather, it is often made up of wounded, worn-out warriors. Many of us in our churches—leaders and members alike—carry weights of buried, unconfessed past sins that we were never meant to carry. Many of us suffer from unhealed emotional wounds that prevent us from responding to situations as the Holy Spirit would like to lead us. Instead, these wounds cause us to respond, consciously or unconsciously, in ways that are influenced or even controlled by our unhealed pain. Many of us are locked into addictions that are ungodly and unseemly, such as gossip, backbiting, dishonesty, pornography, gluttony, outbursts of anger or hate, uncontrollable sex practices, TV, abiding bitterness, and unforgiveness.[1] Many persons, even leaders in the Church, live in the realm of the flesh by being touchy, easily offended, controlling, manipulative, greedy, and proud. Too many are seeking status and man's approval.

The result is that our witness is hindered, both by the adverse appraisal of those outside the Church and by our own inability to speak the power of God to cleanse, heal, and give victory when our own lives are not cleansed, healed, and victorious.

Can this be what God intended? Can this be the Church, able to crash through the very gates of hell? It is my conviction that God intends for His sons and daughters to live power-filled, clean, victorious lives that fully honor Him and that fully reflect the indwelling life of His Son. We may not become perfect in this life, but He draws us to move in that direction. He asks us to put aside "every weight, and the sin which so easily ensnares us" (Heb. 12:1 NKJV).

A Secret

In His kindness and mercy, God has allowed His saints from time to time to discover various keys that open up ways to grow more like Jesus. One of the secrets to a life of consecration and victorious living—with a consequent glorious evangelistic harvest—is God's "empowering presence." This is how it is referred to by Dr. Gordon Fee in his book entitled *Paul, the Spirit, and the People of God,*[2] which is the shortened version of his definitive work on the subject of the Holy Spirit in the writings of the apostle Paul.[3] Dr. Fee is dean at Regent College and is one of the most respected New Testament scholars today. His understanding of

---

1.   It is my experience that such addictions can be demonic. I do not believe that a Christian can be "demon possessed" because possession implies ownership, and we have been purchased by the Lord Jesus Christ. We can, however, be "demonized," which means to be oppressed by evil spirits called demons. I was—until God set me free. When I use the word *deliverance* in this Introduction, I am talking about getting free from the dominating influence of evil spirits, or demons.

2.   Dr. Gordon D. Fee, *Paul, the Spirit, and the People of God* (Peabody, MA: Hendrickson, 1996). Dr. Fee demonstrates that the experience of the power of the Holy Spirit was the most important and foundational tenet of Paul's writings. Even more central to understanding Paul and his theology than "justification by faith" is the experience of God's "empowering presence." In Paul's view, this experience was how one could know that he had been justified by faith.

3.   This larger work is entitled *God's Empowering Presence: The Holy Spirit in the Letters of Paul* (Peabody, MA: Hendrickson, 1994).

Romans 7 has been most encouraging to me personally as an exegetical basis for my belief that Paul did not expect a Christian to be defeated most of the time, but rather to live a life characterized by victory. Paul expected to see victorious lives, not just in periods of great outpourings of the Holy Spirit, but constantly. I am greatly indebted to Dr. Fee for allowing me to reprint Chapter 11 of *Paul, the Spirit, and the People of God* as Chapter 2 of this book. I heartily recommend his entire book to every believer who desires and seeks a more holy life in the here and now.

Similarly, the message of the contributing authors to this book is also that God's empowering presence is available to seeking believers *now, today*! It is that God's desire for us, *today*, is that we move into a life of power, holiness, and evangelism, and that He is well able to do the necessary enabling work in us, *now*.

Some aspects of this empowering are now familiar to us. We have seen some manifestations of the presence of the Holy Spirit and some marvelous accompanying physical and emotional healing and deliverances, usually in the setting of powerful corporate worship. What may not be realized as broadly, though, is that God's power is available to set believers free through the simple process of quietly and sincerely taking the necessary steps in a church or private interview setting.

What does this have to do with evangelism? Much, indeed! I believe that many of us do not evangelize because we are so defeated in our own personal moral lives. Shame over our defeats keeps us from witnessing boldly to the saving power of the gospel. However, when the power of God liberates us, not only from the hell to come but also from the present hell of repeated moral failure, we cannot help telling others of our victory. A person in bondage can never evangelize effectively, no matter how many workshops on evangelism he attends. But when the total truth sets us totally free, we can't help telling others, "Once I was bound, but now I am free!"

Power, Holiness, and Evangelism

This book has a threefold focus, as its title suggests—*power, holiness, and evangelism*. It is about power because without the empowering presence of God, holiness is not possible and our evangelism is feeble at best. It is about holiness because without some degree of holiness, we cannot demonstrate the character of God. Without holiness, evangelism often fails to be very persuasive. It is about evangelism because it is a charge from the Lord Himself and is also the inevitable outgrowth of a life lived in the power, holiness, and joy of God.

Not everyone agrees that a higher degree of holiness is possible or even intended by God. Many of today's evangelical teachers and preachers emphasize a doctrine of imputed righteousness—justification by faith without any expression of hope of experiential righteousness. Now, I too believe in the imputed righteousness of Jesus Christ, which came to me the moment that I was converted. But I also believe that God wants us to have an ever-increasing reality of *experiential* righteousness. I realize that iniquity is part of the fall and that I continually fall short of the glory of God as revealed in Jesus Christ. But I also believe that I can be freed from those of my sins that are driven by demonic pressure on me and that I can be healed of debilitating wounds. Through Christ I can more successfully overcome the temptations that lead to transgressions of the law of God. I have not been perfected, but I have experienced the power of God's grace to stop committing some sins that I had not been able to stop prior to receiving this fresh and powerful experience of God's empowering presence. I am not addressing the subject of justification here, but rather, the subject of sanctification.

Tools for Evangelism

Repentance, deliverance, and inner healing are among the most important tools we have in our Christian walk to assist us in the pursuit of holiness and in becoming equipped for evangelism. I believe sanctification is a lifelong process, but there can be and are experiences or events that greatly advance the process of narrowing the gap between our positional holiness and our experiential holiness. This process can occur over a relatively long period of time, but it can also occur in a relatively brief period of time.

I am not trying to place deliverance and inner healing over and against the traditional Christian disciplines as a means of obtaining holiness and growing in sanctification. I do not believe in substituting them for the time-honored calls to crucifying the flesh, self-denial, and growing in the grace and knowledge of our Lord. However, I do believe that the ministries of deliverance and inner healing should be *added* to the sanctification equation.

Not only have I personally experienced the liberation from certain strongholds in my life, but my ministry team and I have seen this liberation occur in many other lives as well. The experience of one young woman of my acquaintance, a mother of small children and a loyal, sweet servant of the Lord for many years, is not uncommon. She was freed from a stronghold in her life and has now become involved in the ministry of deliverance and inner healing. She described her deliverance and resulting freedom this way: "I had no idea that anyone could live in this freedom, this side of Heaven!"

The Latin American Models

For a number of years now, several cities in Central and South America have been experiencing marvelous fires of revival. In some of these cities, there is a strong deliverance ministry, usually coupled with a ministry that leads individuals through thorough repentance and inner healing. (Interestingly, the question of whether a Christian can be demonized is not even asked any longer in Latin America. There has been so much evidence of demonization among believers, it happens so frequently, and there is so much demonstrated need for inner healing among believers, that it is now part of Latin American theology.)

I once asked the famous Argentinean evangelist Carlos Annacondia why the percentages of new converts from the crusades who actually become disciples are so much higher in South America than in North America.[4] He responded, "Because in North America you give them enough of the gospel to get them forgiven, but not enough to get them free." At his crusades, which have brought some two to three million lost souls into God's Kingdom, after giving an invitation, he does not allow those who have come forward to leave the front immediately. Instead, the altar workers get the needed information for follow-up from the new converts, and then Carlos begins to pray powerfully against the unclean spirits in the people. Many begin to manifest the demonic influences upon them by shaking, falling to the ground, shrieking, or being attacked with severe headaches. Others hear voices saying, "I don't have to come out!" Those who manifest these and similar behaviors or symptoms are taken or carried out to a deliverance tent. There they are ministered to by trained ministry people, many of whom are lay people. Most of these individuals leave having experienced great healing and relief from oppression.

---

4. In Latin America, following the ministry of evangelist Carlos Annacondia, the remaining fruit has been reported as high as 80 percent, while in North America, as most of us know, the success rate has not been nearly as successful.

Pablo Bottari supervised the deliverance tent for Carlos Annacondia for many years. He has personally ministered deliverance to thousands of demonized believers—pastors included—and has supervised workers who have ministered deliverance to more than 60,000 persons. God has given him a model for deliverance that is quiet, dignified, pastoral, and effective. Pablo teaches and preaches extensively in the United States and other countries. He has influenced some of the contributors to this book. A condensed version of a ministry model that is based upon his teaching is included in Chapter 9.

Pablo Deiros and Carlos Mraida co-pastor a large Baptist church in Argentina, the oldest in that country. Dr. Deiros is a professor of Church history at the International Baptist Theological Seminary in Buenos Aires, Argentina. He has also taught at Princeton and Fuller Theological Seminaries in the United States.[5] Their church is actively engaged in the ministries of deliverance and inner healing, and it is a pioneer in developing clinics for pastors and church leaders to help them get free and then teach them to help others get liberated. Carlos Mraida has contributed a chapter on inner healing to this book. Dr. Deiros is a co-contributor with Pablo Bottari in the chapter on deliverance.

Of course, many believers are saved in the local church, rather than in a crusade. Many Latin American churches have worked out a way to see such new believers helped through repentance, deliverance, inner healing, and the baptism in the Holy Spirit. Some have a weekend once a month where all the new converts are gathered together for that purpose. Some of the larger churches, which see hundreds saved in a month, have these weekend meetings more frequently. Caesar Castellanos is the senior pastor of the largest church in the Western hemisphere, located in Bogota, Colombia. His church uses three weekend retreats each month to help make disciples out of new believers, and part of this time is spent in ministering deliverance to them.

---

5.   It is Dr. Deiros' observation, based on considerable experience, that the United States is possibly the nation on earth most affected by demonic oppression. One reason for this may be the fact that our defenses are down, partly due to a belief that a Christian cannot be bothered by demons. I can confirm this. When I began preaching about the need for freedom and the possibility of obtaining freedom in Christ, I was amazed at the percentage of people who began to come forward for prayer upon the invitation for Christians who feel they need to have chains of bondage broken. Usually, it will be from 40 to 60 percent of those present in the meetings.

Thorough repentance, inner healing, and deliverance are major parts of the life of the Latin American Protestant church, whether it is Pentecostal, charismatic, or traditional. In my view, this is an important reason why the evangelical church in Latin America is on such a remarkable growth curve. (See Chapter 5, "Power Evangelism to Reach the Lost.")

The pattern in Latin America of ministering repentance, inner healing, deliverance, and the baptism in the Holy Spirit promptly after the conversion of new believers is impressive. Of course, many churches in North America do not have hundreds saved in a month. They may not have any saved in a month, or even over the course of a few months. It may be that we will not see new conversions on the scale of Latin America for a while. However, perhaps our churches can establish programs in which mature Christians take new believers through these steps informally or individually without a weekend retreat, or perhaps like-minded churches can combine to do a monthly weekend getaway, where all their new converts for that month could get together for ministry.

Where Do We Go From Here?

I am so glad to be alive today, in this day of a wonderful outpouring of the Holy Spirit. I hope that you will be open and sensitive to the Holy Spirit in allowing you to see the underlying theme of this book. It is surely God's will that we be a holy people. Jesus called us to be holy. The apostle Paul wrote to Timothy that God "...has saved us and called us to a holy life—not because of anything we have done but because of His own purpose and grace" (2 Tim. 1:9a). Of course, there are many other injunctions in the Scripture to be holy. It is clear that a holy life is the will of God for us. But, how do we fulfill the apostle Paul's admonition, "As a prisoner for the Lord, then, I urge you to live a life worthy of the calling you have received" (Eph. 4:1).

I believe that living a life worthy of the calling that we have received will surely involve obedience to the will of God as revealed in His moral precepts in the Scripture, especially the Ten Commandments and the Sermon on the Mount. It will involve having a passion for the Triune God and for His Kingdom and His Bride, the Church of Jesus Christ. It will also involve experiencing the power of His presence, which enables us to walk in His holiness with a heart for winning the lost.

Randy Clark
St. Louis, Missouri

Section I

The Biblical Call and Experience

Scott McDermott (Ph.D.) is an adjunct professor at Perkins School of Theology at Southern Methodist University in Texas. He is also the senior pastor at Washington Crossing United Methodist Church in Washington Crossing, Pennsylvania. In 1994 the Lord began to move in power over that congregation, calling the people to deeper personal and corporate prayer, the study of the Bible, vibrant worship, and missions of restoration and revival to the Church and of outreach to the world. Scott's personal passion is to see the Lord bring people into His Kingdom and to see those people equipped and then used by the Lord to reach others.

Chapter 1

The Freedom Cry of Holiness

by Dr. Scott McDermott

Therefore, prepare your minds for action; be self-controlled; set your hope fully on the grace to be given you when Jesus Christ is revealed. As obedient children, do not conform to the evil desires you had when you lived in ignorance. **But just as He who called you is holy, so be holy in all you do; for it is written: "Be holy, because I am holy"** (1 Peter 1:13-16).

Words forgotten? Seldom considered? Perhaps! After all, for some, holiness is associated with matters far removed from the heart. Holiness is considered external, wooden, even legalistic. But as I hope to illustrate in this chapter, nothing could be further from the truth. Far from being external, holiness establishes itself in the heart of the individual. Far from being legalistic, holiness is the freedom cry of a Church delivered and set free from the powers of darkness. In essence, holiness is not *our* agenda, but *God's* agenda, calling all who will listen to the exodus found in His Son to a pathway of new freedom, new life, new power, new purpose, and new hope.

What does it mean to be holy?

The Term *Holy*

When you see the words *holy*, *holiness*, *saints*, *sanctify*, and *consecrate* in the Bible, they usually are translated from Hebrew and Greek word groupings that convey the idea of division, separation, and being set apart.[1] In fact, the Hebrew root of the terms means to cut, to separate. To consider a person, place, or thing *holy* is to consider that object or person set apart *from* the secular, the common, and the profane.

However, holiness not only means to be separated *from* something, it also means to be consecrated *for* something. Holiness defines the purpose for the separation. So, for example, ground is deemed holy; it is the place where God has chosen to reveal His name (see Ex. 3:5). The city of Jerusalem is holy, for it is the place where God will commune with His people (see Neh. 11:1). The temple furnishings are holy because they are set apart as instruments of worship and praise to God. What makes all these things holy is the fact that God has deemed them as set apart *from* that which is common, secular, and profane, and set aside *for* His purposes.[2]

God Is Holy

God is able to make a holy claim upon people, places, and things because God Himself is holy. Take, for example, these words from the Psalms:

> *Let them praise Your great and awesome name—**He is holy**....Exalt the Lord our God and worship at His footstool; **He is holy** (Psalm 99:3,5).*

The apostle John also informs us that the four creatures around the throne are constantly proclaiming the holiness of the Lord.

> *...Day and night they never stop saying: "Holy, holy, holy is the Lord God Almighty, who was, and is, and is to come" (Revelation 4:8).*

What do these descriptions tell us about God? They testify that "holiness" best describes the essential character and nature of God. God is all holy, indicating His majesty and transcendence. He is completely

---

1. Richard Whitaker, ed., *The Abridged Brown-Driver-Briggs Hebrew-English Lexicon of the Old Testament*, CD-ROM (Oak Harbor, WA: Logos Research Systems, Inc., 1997), Hebrew קדשׁ. See also Walter Bauer, F. Wilbur Gingrich, and Frederick W. Danker, *A Greek-English Lexicon of the New Testament and Other Early Christian Literature*, CD-ROM (Oak Harbor, WA: Logos Research Systems, Inc., 1997), Greek ἅγιος.
2. Horst Seebas, "Holy," *The New International Dictionary of New Testament Theology*, Colin Brown, ed. (Grand Rapids: Zondervan, 1976), 223.

apart from what is sinful and finite.[3] As Thomas Oden states: "The moral quality that best points to God's incomparable good character, as one incomparable in power, is holiness, for holiness (*godesh*) implies that every excellence fitting to the Supreme Being is found in God without blemish or limit."[4]

But what is most interesting in the Scripture is the way in which God acts to reproduce His holiness and character in the lives of those who seek Him. Indeed the Old and New Testaments echo this theme.

> *Consecrate yourselves and be holy, because I am the Lord your God. Keep My decrees and follow them. I am the Lord,* **who makes you holy** (Leviticus 20:7-8).

Also in Exodus 31:13, in discussion of the keeping of the Sabbath, we find the same declaration:

> *Say to the Israelites, "You must observe My Sabbaths. This will be a sign between Me and you for the generations to come, so you may know that I am the Lord,* **who makes you holy.**"

The New Testament Book of Hebrews echoes the same message.

> *In bringing many sons to glory, it was fitting that God, for whom and through whom everything exists, should make the author of their salvation perfect through suffering.* **Both the one who makes men holy and those who are made holy** *are of the same family...* (Hebrews 2:10-11).

God makes His holiness known so that we too may be made holy. In fact, although the New International Version translates all these passages as "who makes you holy," the phrase can literally be translated, "who sanctifies you." *Sanctification* is the act of making a person, place, or thing holy. People, places, and things are set apart from their former use and purpose for another use and purpose.

The calling of the prophet Isaiah is perhaps one of the best examples of God's acting to sanctify someone for His tasks.

> *In the year that King Uzziah died, I saw the Lord seated on a throne, high and exalted, and the train of His robe filled the temple. Above Him were seraphs, each with six wings: With two wings they covered*

---

3. Raymond E. Brown, Joseph A. Fitzmyer, and Roland E. Murphy, eds., *Jerome Biblical Commentary* (Englewood Cliffs, NJ: Prentice Hall, 1968). See Isaiah 6 discussion.
4. Thomas Oden, *The Living God: Systematic Theology*, Vol. I (San Francisco: Harper, 1992), 99.

their faces, with two they covered their feet, and with two they were fly-ing. And they were calling to one another: "Holy, holy, holy is the Lord Almighty; the whole earth is full of His glory." At the sound of their voices the doorposts and thresholds shook and the temple was filled with smoke. "Woe to me!" I cried. "I am ruined! For I am a man of unclean lips, and I live among a people of unclean lips, and my eyes have seen the King, the Lord Almighty." Then one of the ser-aphs flew to me with a live coal in his hand, which he had taken with tongs from the altar. With it he touched my mouth and said, "See, this has touched your lips; your guilt is taken away and your sin atoned for." Then I heard the voice of the Lord saying, "Whom shall I send? And who will go for Us?" And I said, "Here am I. Send me!" (Isaiah 6:1-8)

Isaiah's words are dramatic indeed. The Lord is revealed as "high and exalted." The doorposts are shaking, thresholds are quaking, and the temple is filled with smoke. The language of the passage reflects the transcendent nature and sovereignty of God and His splendor, power, and separation from that which is ordinary and profane. The grandeur of the vision is enhanced with the picture of the seraphs flying around the throne proclaiming, "holy, holy, holy." Using the word *holy* three times is a biblical way of indicating holiness in the superlative. There is no one holy like the Lord.

No wonder Isaiah exclaimed "Woe to me" and "I am ruined." Isa-iah recognized his unworthiness and the unworthiness of the people of his generation. But, just as we noted above, God acts to sanctify, to set apart, to separate, and therefore, to make holy. One of the seraphs flew to Isaiah, took a live coal from the altar, and touched his lips with it. With this action, Isaiah is cleansed. He is separated *from* his sin. In fact, the seraph announced, "Your guilt is taken away and your sin atoned for." However, as we see in the passage, the Holy God acts not only to separate Isaiah from his sin but also to set Isaiah aside *for* His purposes. Isaiah is set apart for the purpose of proclaiming the message of holiness to the nation. Just as Isaiah was cleansed by the Holy God, so too must Israel be cleansed. As one scholar notes, "Israel and Judah will not be able to experience the lovingkindness of the Lord until they have been cleansed and sanctified; only then can they experience the presence of the Holy One of Israel."[5]

---

5.   Walter A. Elwell, ed., *Evangelical Commentary on the Bible* (Grand Rapids: Baker Book House Company, 1989), CD-ROM. See Isaiah 6 discussion.

In this season of worldwide revival, it is not uncommon to hear testimonies of the revelation of God's holiness, and with it, the keen sense of one's unworthiness, and yet the powerful revelation that God extends forgiveness and even a sanctifying touch. Recently a member of our United Methodist congregation, Joe Sullivan, had such an experience. Oh, I am sure it was not on the level of Isaiah's vision, but this encounter with the Lord had a "setting apart" aftereffect. Read of the way in which he describes how God acted out of majesty to do a work of setting apart in his life:

> "I started wailing on the floor of the auditorium like I never knew before. What I knew from Scripture in my head penetrated to my soul, spirit, and body. Truth pervaded every fiber of my being. I now knew God's sovereignty and majesty. I could feel His Abba daddy love for me, truth that I am a joint heir with Christ and was given authority to represent Him on earth just blew me away. I felt so unworthy, yet worth was imputed to me. All this was causing me to wail from the depths of my being."

Joe notes that this experience went on for about an hour. As I talked with Joe recently, I could sense the newfound tranquility in his life. Some deep issues had been resolved with him, a newfound strength was there for him, and more importantly, he knew in his heart, not just his head, that God had made him to be set apart for His purposes.

Although all our experiences with the Lord may not be as intense as the one Joe experienced, God has, in Christ, sanctified and set apart all who acknowledge Him. In the Scriptures, this act of sanctification is presented as both a past event and a present process. Let's consider for a moment the past event of sanctification.

Sanctification as a Life-Altering Event

God has acted in Christ to set apart those who seek Him. You may find it surprising that the Scriptures refer to a believer's sanctification as a past event. Paul, for example, refers to the Corinthians as those who have been "sanctified in Christ" (1 Cor. 1:2). Later, Paul states in First Corinthians 6:11, "...But you were washed, you were *sanctified*, you were justified in the name of the Lord Jesus Christ and by the Spirit of our God." From these references, and others as well, we may conclude that sanctification is a past event. It is something that has already occurred.

But this conclusion raises an important question: "In what way have we been sanctified?"

As we noted above, to be sanctified means that a person, place, or thing has been set apart *from* that which is secular, profane, or common and set aside *for* a holy purpose. What are the things that believers have been set aside from? The Scriptures tell us that believers are set apart from the kingdom of darkness (see Acts 26:18), from the agenda and paradigm of life derived from the world (see Rom. 3:6,19; 1 Cor. 1:20,27f; 2 Cor. 5:19), and from the power of sin and death (see Rom. 6–8). All this occurs because the believer derives his or her existence from being "in Christ," not from the dominion of darkness, the world, or one's own fleshly existence. In effect, a separation has occurred from one's old way of life, and the new has come (see 2 Cor. 5:17).

In particular, one who is in Christ is set apart for God. That is, he who believes in Christ is set apart to do the will of the Father in the world (see Mt. 6:9-10). As those who do the Father's will, God's people are called to share the message of His good news in Christ (see Mt. 28:18-20), to spread His grace and love (see Gal. 5:22), and to do His good works (see Eph. 2:10). This is precisely what Paul means when he states that the Corinthians have been sanctified. They have been set apart from their old ways and set aside for God's divine purpose.

Does this mean that a believer no longer sins or is perfect in every way? Far from it! But now in Christ believers live under a new rule and a new power. Indeed, they have new purpose for their lives.

It seems to be that in this age of revival, God is once again challenging His Church with the message of sanctification. He is showing us how far we have fallen from the call of holiness that He has placed over His people. Recently a group of people from our church went to a distant country to encourage and minister to missionaries serving in that land. Their travels took them to one of the world's most polluted metropolitan areas. JoAnn Muller shares her reflections:

> "During our day trip to one of the world's most polluted cities, we found the air thick with toxins that caused our throats and noses to burn, even when we covered them. The smell of the pollutants didn't seem to affect the people living in that country. Their response was, 'You get used to it.' The Lord spoke to me clearly about His Church and the compromise of His people having allowed the worldly pollutants to creep into her.

Over time, we have grown to accept them and no longer are we repulsed by their stench. But a Holy God cannot come close into fellowship with us until we repent of the toxins that have polluted the purity of the gospel and its truth. Therefore, we have little to no power because God wants to establish His presence in a place of purity.

"Until we recognize the impurities that we have embraced in our 'houses of prayer,' which are not the buildings we call churches, but rather, our hearts, we will not see the demonstration of God's power and the glory we have longed for. We are called to be living sacrifices, holy, and pleasing unto God, with no compromise of His standards, His Truth, or His definition of holiness."

Just as the Corinthians were called "sanctified," and on the basis of that designation were called to repent of their compromised attitudes and lifestyles, so also God is reminding the Church that she too is sanctified and must change the way that she lives.

God, therefore, uses the past event of sanctification as an invitation to join Him in the ongoing process of our sanctification. You may ask, "How can sanctification be both a past and present event?" Perhaps marriage serves as a way of illustrating this concept. On their wedding day, the bride and groom make exclusive claims and commitments to each other. On that day, they each commit before God, friends, and family that they will love, honor, and cherish each other through all of life's circumstances. Most importantly, they make the commitment that they will now keep themselves exclusively for their spouse for as long as they both shall live. This commitment is an act of sanctification, an act of setting apart, and an act of newly defined purpose. However, though sanctified and set apart for each other, this couple will now need to learn to live out what they have already committed to, and what God and the state recognize they are; that is, married, set apart as a couple. They now involve themselves in the marriage process.

So God invites us to join in the process of sanctification, that is, the living out of what He has already done in Christ for us.

Sanctification as a Present Process

In fact, one way in which God involves us in the process of our sanctification is through the power of prayer. When Jesus teaches His disciples to pray, He teaches them to pray in this way: "Our Father in heaven, hallowed be Your name" (Mt. 6:9). To pray for the hallowing of God's name means more than just honoring the name of God; it also means that the name of the Lord is to be glorified through obedience to His will and commands. As Colin Brown states, "The petitions are a cry from the depths of distress. From a world enslaved by evil, death, and Satan, the disciples are to lift their eyes to the Father and cry out for the revelation of his glory, knowing in faith he will grant it."[6]

The prayer for the revelation of the holiness of God in creation is, then, the *freedom cry* of the Church. For in crying out for the hallowing of God's name, one prays for the eradication of all that is contrary to God's will and commands, including those things in his life that are contrary to His will.[7]

This freedom cry will have an effect upon the ways of our heart and upon the way in which we live.

A Transformation of Heart

First of all, it is important to understand that sanctification is an inside job. True holiness begins with the holiness of the heart. Not surprisingly, the Bible places great significance upon the heart. Consider, for example, the counsel given in the Book of Proverbs.

Above all else, guard your heart, for it is the wellspring of life (Proverbs 4:23).

Jesus also gave clear instructions in the Gospel of Matthew:

Don't you see that whatever enters the mouth goes into the stomach and then out of the body? But the things that come out of the mouth come from the heart, and these make a man "unclean." For out of the heart come evil thoughts, murder, adultery, sexual immorality, theft, false testimony, slander. These are what make a man "unclean"; but eating with unwashed hands does not make him "unclean" (Matthew 15:17-20).

Why all this emphasis upon the heart? Because the heart consists not only of emotions but also of thoughts and understanding and the realm of the will and choice. Now think about that for a moment. When Proverbs instructs us to guard our hearts, it is stating that we are to

---

6. Seebas, "Holy," *The New International Dictionary of New Testament Theology*, Brown, ed., 229.
7. Seebas, "Holy," *The New International Dictionary of New Testament Theology*, Brown, ed., 229.

guard our emotions, our thoughts and understanding, and our choices. When Jesus states that the things that come out of a man's heart are what defiles him and makes him unclean, He is stating that such a person has surrendered his emotions, thoughts, and choices to that which is unclean. What comes out of a person is a reflection of what is already inside.

As people who are set apart in Christ, our hearts are no longer to be captive to the choices of our flesh and human passions, nor are we to live in captivity to the ways of the world and its agenda upon our lives (see Rom. 12:1-2). Rather, as believers, we are called to a greater, higher way of life:

> ... *"Love the Lord your God with all your heart and with all your soul and with all your mind." This is the first and greatest commandment* (Matthew 22:37-38).

At times in our worship services we will see the Lord move in people's hearts in some wonderful ways. God is making His purposes known to those who call upon Him, revealing to them that they are set apart from a worldly and purely fleshly agenda. He is making known His claim upon the passions, desires, intentions, and understandings of the heart. Little wonder people roll upon the floor when they see their heart, their wounds, their wrong choices, and their sin. Sometimes our hearts are not a pretty sight.

I find it helpful to regularly come before the Lord and ask Him to show me my heart. I reflect upon my feelings, my thoughts, my choices, and my understanding. I have found that this is one prayer God answers immediately. Not always, but rather regularly, I will write down what I see in my heart and the way in which the Lord ministers to me. He has always been faithful.

In addition to changing our hearts, the freedom cry of the Church for the hallowing of God's name will also affect the way in which we live.

A Change of Lifestyle

In Romans 12:1-2, Paul called the Romans to a lifestyle that flows out of a life of sacrifice to God.

> *Therefore, I urge you, brothers, in view of God's mercy, to offer your bodies as living sacrifices, holy and pleasing to God—this is your spiritual act of worship. Do not conform any longer to the pattern of this world, but be transformed by the renewing of your mind. Then you*

will be able to test and approve what God's will is—His good, pleasing and perfect will.

To offer a sacrifice is to acknowledge "the preeminence of God above all social statuses, the admission that God is the one who controls all—hence a broad symbol of honor, submission and obedience...."[8] Believers no longer offer animals as a sacrifice; rather they are now to offer themselves, their bodies, and hence all their conduct and behavior as sacrifices to God.[9] In First Corinthians, Paul calls into question the improper sexual behavior among the Corinthians and states,

> *Do you not know that your body is a temple of the Holy Spirit, who is in you, whom you have received from God? You are not your own; you were bought at a price. Therefore honor God with your body* (1 Corinthians 6:19-20).

Believers are called to offer their own personal moral conduct as well as their social interactions to God as a sacrifice acceptable to Him.

It is wonderful to see how the Lord graciously cleans up the lives of those who have fallen. It is not uncommon to hear the confessions of those who have fallen through their own wrong choices. I have watched them work through their pain in honest confession and repentance, and I have seen them step into areas of accountability with another brother or sister so that they will not fall again. God's grace in the lives of these believers has truly been amazing.

On one of our men's retreats, the Lord began to move over our men in areas of sexual brokenness and sexual sins. At the ministry time, you could hear the sounds of men weeping as they openly confessed the secrets of their hearts and repented of the sin that had woven its way into the fabric of their souls. At times their prayers were a simple and gentle affirmation of the freedom that Christ had wrought for them on Calvary. At other times the prayers were more forceful and loud. Freedom was now becoming their heart cry. What began on that evening almost two years ago has continued to bear fruit in the lives of these men. In fact, many of the married men went home and confessed their sins to their wives, asked their forgiveness, and requested that their wives hold them accountable for the areas where their lives had become vulnerable to temptation. But that is not all. A good number of these men became

---

8.   Bruce Malina, *The New Testament World: Insights from Cultural Anthropology* (Atlanta: John Knox Press, 1981), 142.

9.   Malina, *New Testament World*, 147.

involved in small groups with other men in order to continue upon the pathway of freedom. The fruit has been remarkable. God changes lives!

I have seen the Lord convict in areas of personal affronts and bitterness, and I have watched the Lord heal lives, heal marriages, and give hope for a future. There is little wonder the Bible calls us to live in the Spirit. In truth, the Scriptures call us to walk in the Spirit (see Gal. 5:16 KJV), pray in the Spirit (see 1 Cor. 14:15), and bear the fruit of the Spirit (see Gal. 5:22ff), all of which have a great deal to do with issues of character and relationships. God sets His will and purpose for our good, for our freedom, and for the betterment of our personal lives and relationships. Our God is for us and not against us.

In joining in this heart cry, the believer is saying to the Lord, "Oh, how I need You. You alone are the source of transformation and change. Only by You can my life know the victory that I need." Holiness and sanctification are the heart cry of the Church because holiness is the agenda of God for His people. We are not called to a holiness that is external, wooden, and legalistic, but to a holiness that is alive, because it gives expression to the heart of God for His Church. In holiness, God's people experience the setting apart of life for a greater divine purpose and will. In holiness, God's people are set free, made new, and welcomed into the ranks of those who are being changed from glory to glory.

Dr. Gordon D. Fee is Professor of New Testament at Regent College, Vancouver, B.C., Canada, where he also serves as Dean of Faculty. A noted New Testament scholar, he has published numerous books and articles, including a textbook on New Testament interpretation and a major work on the Holy Spirit in the letters of Paul. Currently he serves as the general editor of the New International Commentary series, succeeding the late F.F. Bruce. Well-known for his manifest concern for the renewal of the Church, Dr. Fee is also an ordained minister with the Assemblies of God.

Chapter 2*

The Ongoing Warfare—The Spirit Against the Flesh

by Dr. Gordon D. Fee

*The Spirit-flesh conflict in Paul has to do not with
an internal conflict in one's soul, but with the
people of God living the life of the future
in a world where the flesh is still very active.*

A good friend wrote recently, "Christians seem to me to divide into
two groups these days: the first lot don't think that sin matters very much
anyway, and the second know perfectly well that it does, but still can't
kick the habit."[1] This chapter picks up the concern of the second lot.
Indeed, we now come to the real world! Painfully, for many of God's
people the subject of this chapter tells the story of their Christian life, a
story of ongoing inner conflict of soul. They take some comfort in believing that Paul was their companion in this struggle. If Paul, the great apostle of the faith, could write, "what I want to do I do not do, but what I

---

* This chapter is a reprint of Chapter 11, "The Ongoing Warfare—The Spirit Against
the Flesh," from Gordon Fee's book, *Paul, the Spirit, and the People of God* (Peabody,
MA: Hendrickson Publishers, 1996). Reprinted by permission. All rights reserved.

1. N.T. Wright, *Following Jesus: Biblical Reflections on Discipleship* (London: SPCK,
1994), 72.

hate I do" (Rom 7:15), then what hope is there for us? So they simply resign themselves to the struggle.

People come by this comfort by reading Galatians 5:17, the single Pauline text that speaks about a *conflict* between the Spirit and the flesh, in light of Romans 7:14-25—although the Spirit is not so much as mentioned in the Romans passage, where Paul describes the conflict that goes on in the soul of a person living under law and without the Spirit's help. People accept this unfortunate reading of Paul at face value, because the text in Romans vividly describes something they know only too well. Sadly, for the vast majority of those who adopt such a view, the flesh usually wins. Thus Paul's passion, namely, the sufficiency of the Spirit for all of life in the present age, is brushed aside as unrealistic in favor of one's own personal reality.

To be sure, such war does rage in the hearts of many. Often the warfare—and the sense of helplessness to live above it—is the direct result of the intense individualism of Western culture. Both secular psychology and much Christian teaching focus on the inner self: How am I doing according to some set of criteria for wholeness? Focused on the inner struggle, we can scarcely see Christ or walk confidently in the way of the Spirit. Instead of living out the fruit of the Spirit, in constant thankfulness for what the Spirit is doing in our lives and in the lives of others, our individualistic faith turns sourly narcissistic—aware of our personal failures before God, frustrated at our imperfections, feigning the love, joy, peace, and gentleness we wish were real. Our turmoil crowds out openness to the Spirit himself. In such spiritual malaise God almost always gets the blame.

But as real as this is for some, Paul is not addressing this issue when in Galatians 5:17 he speaks of the Spirit and "flesh" as in utter opposition to each other. Indeed, he would not even understand it. His world is that of Psalm 19, not that of "the introspective conscience of the West."[2] In consecutive verses (12-13), the psalmist acknowledges first his "errors" and "hidden faults" and then the possibility of "willful sins." The former is an acknowledgment of the depth of our fallenness; for these "hidden faults" he asks forgiveness. His concern—and it does not take the form of a struggle—is with the "willful sins." About these he prays that they will "not rule over me."[3] Paul's view is similar. In Galatians 5:17

---

2.   These words come from Krister Stendahl, "The Apostle Paul and the Introspective Conscience of the West," in *Paul Among Jews and Gentiles and Other Essays* (Philadelphia: Fortress, 1976), 78-96.

3.   See also Ps 51, where David speaks of his "sin as ever before me" (v. 3) and of his having "done what is evil" (v. 4). But he also knows the source of such sin, the evil heart, which he refers to in vv. 5-6.

he is not addressing a struggle over "hidden faults" but open disobedience to God in the form of "willful sins."

At issue for us in this chapter, therefore, is Paul's own view of the conflict between the Spirit and the flesh, between living *kata sarka* ("according to the flesh") and *kata pneuma* ("according to the Spirit"). Every occurrence of these terms in Paul has to do with our present eschatological existence—what it means for believers to live *together as a people*, defined by the already/not yet fulfillment of God's promises, in contrast to a former life defined and determined by the world. My point: Nowhere does Paul describe Christian life, life in the Spirit, as one of constant struggle with the flesh.[4] He simply does not speak to that question. His point rather is the sufficiency of the Spirit for God's new end-time people.

Basic to Paul's view is that, as with Torah observance, the time of the flesh is over for followers of Christ. According to Romans 7:4-6, Christ and the Spirit have, with the new covenant, brought an end to the time of the law and the flesh, which belong to our existence *before* and *outside* Christ. Continuing to live this way is incompatible with life "according to the Spirit" (Rom 8:5-8). But Paul's view does not represent triumphalism, as though people who lived by the Spirit were never tempted by the old life in the flesh or that they never succumbed to such. They have, and they do; and there is forgiveness for such, and gracious restoration.

A careful analysis of the key texts Galatians 5:17 and Romans 7:14-25 demonstrates that this is Paul's perspective. But we will be helped in that analysis by looking first at Paul's use of the term "flesh."[5]

The Meaning of "Flesh" in Paul

The place to begin such a study is with the Old Testament, since Paul's usage originates there. The Hebrew word *bāśār* refers primarily to the flesh of bodies, and by derivation sometimes to the bodies themselves. On a few occasions the term is extended to describe human frailty and creatureliness, usually in contrast to God as creator. Thus a common expression for all living beings, especially humans, is "all flesh," meaning "every creature." When the psalmist asks in light of his trust in God,

---

4.   See the discussion in *GEP* [*God's Empowering Presence*] of Gal 5:13-15, 16-17, 19-23, 24-26; 6:7-10; Rom 7:4-6; 8:4, 5-8; 13:11-14; Phil 3:3.

5.   For further reference to recent scholarship on this question, especially the position of J.D.G. Dunn, to which some of the following is a response, see Fee, *GEP*, 816-22.

"What can flesh do to me?" (Ps 56:4), he means that with God as his pro-
tector what can a mere human do to him (cf. Jer 17:5). In his anguish Job
asks God, "Do you have eyes of flesh? Do you see as humans see?" While
"flesh" is not a neutral term when used in this way, neither does it
express a negative moral judgment; rather, it expresses the frailty of
human creatureliness. It would be unthinkable to the Hebrew that sin lay
in the flesh, since sin's origins lie in the human heart.

Although Paul rarely uses the Greek term *sarx* in its basic sense, as
referring to the physical body, he regularly uses it in the extended sense
as referring to our humanity in some way or another. Thus he can speak
of "Israel according to the flesh" (1 Cor 10:18), or Abraham as our fore-
father "according to the flesh" (Rom 4:1), or of Jesus as descended from
David "according to the flesh" (Rom 1:3), meaning in each case "according to ordinary human descent." In the same mode Paul recognizes present human life as still "in the flesh" (e.g., Gal 2:20; 2 Cor 10:3), that is,
lived out in the present human body, characterized by frailty as it is.

Paul also uses *sarx*, however, in a more unusual sense, derived in
part from intertestamental Judaism, but marked by his own basically
eschatological view of life in the world. "Flesh" for him denotes humanity not simply in its creatureliness vis-à-vis God, but in its *fallen* creatureliness as utterly hostile to God in every imaginable way. It is in this sense
that he contrasts life "according to the flesh" over against life "according
to the Spirit." The one describes the present evil age in terms of human
fallenness, where by nature each has turned to his or her own way; the
other describes the eschatological age that has dawned with the coming
of Christ and the Spirit, as described in chapter 5 above.

This does not make *sarx* an easy term to translate. The NIV often uses
"sinful nature."[6] That translation works well in Romans 7, where Paul is
describing the failure of his former life under the law. The "flesh" represents "another law in his members" that rises up to defeat the law of God
and thus to render the law helpless. That "other law" is his own "sinful
nature." But this rendering does not work well in other places, where he
is describing what characterizes the whole world in its present fallenness.

The clearest instance in which Paul plays on the two basic senses of
this word ("human frailty" and "human fallenness") is in 2 Corinthians

---

6.   But does so inconsistently. It uses "sinful nature" when "flesh" implies a negative
      moral judgment (e.g., see 1 Cor 5:5; Gal 5:13, 16, 17 [twice], 19, 24; 6:8; Rom
      7:5–8:13; Col 2:11, 13; Eph 2:3), but "worldly point of view" in 2 Cor 5:16 (cf. 1:12,
      17; 10:2) and "flesh" in Phil 3:3–4!

10:2-4. Accused by them of acting "according to the flesh" in the morally negative sense, Paul allows, for the sake of his argument, that he does indeed live "*in* the flesh," by which he means "in the weaknesses and limitations of present mortality." But, he goes on, I do not engage in warfare "*according to* the flesh," in keeping with the fallenness which characterizes the present age that, because of the cross and resurrection, is on its way out. This argument does not work at all if "flesh" is morally negative in both instances.

Our interest lies strictly with this latter sense, human fallenness, which has completely lost its relationship to the physical and has become strictly eschatological—and morally negative—describing existence from the perspective of those who do not know Christ, who thus live as God's enemies. It describes believers only *before* they came to be in Christ and live by the Spirit. Any conflict in this matter has to do with believers in Christ, people of the Spirit, continuing to behave according to their pre-Christ perspective and values. Paul's point always is, "Stop it." "Put off your old self," he says, and "put on the new self" (Eph 4:22, 24). My point, then, is that whenever "flesh" occurs in contrast to the Spirit, it always bears this eschatological sense.

The Spirit-Flesh Contrast in Paul[7]

That Paul viewed the flesh as belonging to the past for believers, in the same way as he viewed Torah observance, is specifically stated in Romans 7:4-6: "When we *were* living in the flesh, the passions of sin, aroused by the law, *were* [also] at work in us;...but now, by dying to what once bound us, we have been set free...to walk in the new way of the Spirit." How Paul understands this is set forth vividly in 2 Corinthians 5:14-17:

> For Christ's love compels us, because we are convinced that one died
> for all, and therefore all died. And he died for all, that those who live
> should no longer live for themselves but for him who died for them
> and was raised again. So then, from now on we regard no one from
> the perspective of the flesh. If indeed we once considered even Christ
> from this perspective, now we know him in this way no longer. So

---

7.   This contrast does not occur nearly as often as we are sometimes led to believe, being found basically in Gal 5:13–6:10 (cf. the analogy in 4:29); Rom 8:3-17; and Phil 3:3–although see also 1 Cor 3:1.

then, if anyone is in Christ, a new creation; the old things have passed away; behold, the new have come.

The death and resurrection of Christ and the gift of the Spirit have changed everything. The former order of things is described in terms of flesh, that basically self-centered, creature-oriented point of view, which has caused the Corinthians to regard Paul as he had formerly regarded Christ, as weak and therefore not of God. The flesh perceives things from the old age point of view, where value and significance lie in power, influence, wealth, and wisdom (cf. 1 Cor 1:26-31).

To be sure, such a worldview is still about. But for those in Christ, all of that has passed away; behold, the new has come, the time of the Spirit, in which there has been a total change in the definition of what has value or significance. The new model is the cross: the power lies not in externals but in the Spirit, who indwells believers and by grace is renewing the "inner person" (2 Cor 4:16), transforming us into God's own likeness (ultimately portrayed in Christ through the cross).

This eschatological view of the Spirit/flesh contrast is found in other passages as well:

1. "I could not speak to you as Spiritual, but as fleshly," Paul tells the Corinthians (1 Cor 3:1). The irony of this sentence lies in the fact that the Corinthians, who think of themselves as Spirit people, are thinking just as they did before they met Christ, just like those leaders of this passing age, who crucified Christ (2:6-8). Their attitude toward Paul's suffering and his message of the cross in effect makes them bedfellows with those who killed Christ, viewing things from the perspective of the flesh.

This is obviously eschatological terminology. Moreover, it does not reflect some internal struggle in the believer between these two kinds of existence. On the contrary, it describes the essential characteristics of the two ages, which exist side by side in unrelieved opposition in our present already but not yet existence. The one, flesh, has been condemned and is on its way out; they are to be done with that. Paul is cajoling them to live the real life of the Spirit.

2. Similarly, in Philippians 3:3 Paul warns against those who would insist on circumcision. He describes believers as those who serve "by the Spirit of God" and who put no confidence in "the flesh." Here "flesh" refers to self-confidence based on a presumed advantaged relationship with God evidenced by circumcision. But as noted in chapter 9 above, the Spirit also stands opposed to, by fulfillment, any form of Torah observance. Thus these too are basically eschatological realities. To revert to circumcision, that is, to put "confidence in the flesh," is to go

back to the way that has come to an end with the death and resurrection of Christ and the gift of the Spirit.

3. The strong contrasts in Romans 8:5-8 likewise do not deal with internal conflict. Paul is again describing the two kinds of existence, and indicating their utter incompatibility. Those who walk according to the flesh—and it is clear in context that this does *not* mean believers, but those still outside Christ—"have their minds set on what the flesh desires" (v. 5). Such a mind-set is hostile to God, does not—indeed, cannot—submit to God's law, cannot please God (how in the world could it?), and ends up in death. That simply does not describe Christian life, not in Paul and not anywhere else.

The people of God, who walk according to the Spirit, live in bold contrast to flesh-walkers. Their minds are set on the things of the Spirit (their minds have been renewed by the Spirit, after all); in place of hostility to God, they live in peace; and instead of death, they know life.

That this is the conflict Paul describes is made certain in Romans 8:9, where he addresses his Christian readers: "but *you*," he says, "are *not in the flesh* [in the sense that the flesh-walkers in vv. 7-8 are], but in the Spirit [a whole new way of existence], since indeed the Spirit of God dwells in you."

But Paul also recognizes that life in the Spirit is not just a stroll in the park. So in Romans 8:12-13 he applies all of vv. 1-11 to their lives, by reminding them that by the Spirit they must continue to kill that to which they have already died (the already/not yet again). They were formerly controlled by, and thus under obligation to, the flesh. Their new obligation is to the Spirit, to walk in his ways, led by him (v. 14).

Life in the Spirit is not passive; nor is obedience automatic. We continue to live in the real world; we are, after all, both already and not yet. Therefore, the imperative for the already is walk in/by the Spirit. That assumes that we live in a world very much controlled by the flesh; but it also assumes that we now live in that world as different people, led by the Spirit and empowered by the Spirit to produce the fruit of righteousness, rather than to continue in the works of the flesh.

That leads us finally to Galatians 5:17 and Romans 7:13-25. We begin with the latter, since it does not have to do with this contrast at all; and conclude by another look at the Galatians passage (see ch. 10 above).

The Struggle in Romans 7:13-25

What about the intense, deeply emotional narration of Paul's own internal conflict in Romans 7:13-25? Doesn't this passage suggest that Paul himself, even though a man of the Spirit, continually struggled in his inner person with the pull of the flesh? At first glance, and taking the passage out of context, one might think so. But three things reveal otherwise: the surrounding context, what Paul actually says, and what he does not say.

The context throughout has to do with the place of Torah in the Christian life. In vv. 1-6 Paul has made it clear, by repeating himself yet one more time, that the believer has no relationship to it at all. In the death of Christ we have died with respect to the law (v. 4). Not only so, he adds, but we have also died with respect to the flesh (vv. 5-6; note the past tense, "when we *were* in the flesh"). But Paul is also aware that he has been extremely hard on the law in his argument to this point, which will hardly sit well with his readers who are Jewish Christians. Besides, he does not really consider the law a bad thing—quite the contrary. His problem with the law was with its inadequacy, its helplessness to empower what it required.

So in vv. 7-25, he sets out to exonerate the law from any suggestion that, because it was implicated in our death, the law itself was a bad thing. To make this point, he argues in two ways. First, he says in vv. 7-12, what killed "me" (and "me" in this paragraph stands for all other Jews as well as for himself) was not the law but the innate sinfulness that the law aroused. The law is implicated in his "death," to be sure, but as an abettor, not as a direct cause.

This, too, could put the law in a bad light, so he starts all over again (v. 13), this time insisting that the law is not really to blame at all. Its fault lay in its helplessness to do anything about the sin it has aroused in us by making us vividly aware of sin's utter "sinfulness." This is said with great intensity, and in a way in which all who try to please God on the basis of law can empathize. In the final analysis it is a totally useless struggle. For the person under law, who has not experienced the gift of the Spirit, sin and the flesh are simply the stronger powers.

Enter Christ and the Spirit (Rom 8), as God's response to the anguished cry of 7:24. Not only is there no condemnation in Christ (that is, the judgment we all so richly deserve has been put into our past through the death of Christ), but we now live by a new "law," that of the Spirit of life (8:2). What the law was unable to do, Christ has now done for us (positionally) and the Spirit "fulfills" in us (experientially) as we "walk in the Spirit" (vv. 3-4).

Three simple points, then, in conclusion:

1. What Paul describes throughout is what it was like to live under the law; and whatever else is true of the Christian Paul, he did not consider himself to be under the law. What he describes, from his now Christian perspective, is what it was like to live under law before Christ and the Spirit. The use of "I" and the present tense of the verbs only heighten the intensity of his feelings toward the utter helplessness of the law to do anything about the real problem of sin.

2. The person here described never wins. Being under the helpless law, in the face of the more powerful flesh and sin, means to be sold as a slave under sin, and thus incapable of doing the good thing the law demands. Such a description is absolutely incompatible with Paul's view of life in Christ, empowered by the Spirit.

3. There is not a single mention of the Spirit in the entire passage (vv. 7-25). The Spirit was last mentioned in v. 6, as the key to our new life in Christ, who has brought our relationship with the law and the flesh to an end. Christ and the Spirit are then picked up again in 8:1-2 as the divine response to the anguished cry of the person struggling with sin, but with the helpless law standing by, pointing out the sinfulness of our sin, unable to do anything about it.

Thus the only questions Paul himself raises in this entire passage have to do with Torah, whether it is good or evil, and, once this is affirmed as good, how this good thing is still implicated in our death. Life under Torah alone is under scrutiny.

Galatians 5:17 in Context

But what of Galatians 5:17, where Paul says (literally), "for the flesh has desires over against the Spirit, and the Spirit over against the flesh; for these two [realities] are in opposition to each other, so that whatever things you may wish [= feel like doing], these things you may not do"? Does this not indicate that there is an internal struggle of the Spirit against the flesh? In context, not so. In fact, this text is precisely in keeping with the texts previously looked at, where this contrast appears.

Verse 17 comes at the heart of an argument dealing with one urgent question: Since Torah observance is now a thing of the past because of the coming of Christ and the Spirit, what is to ensure righteousness? That is, Paul is arguing against (perhaps anticipating) Jewish

Christian opposition that would see his bypassing Torah observance as a sure invitation to license and ungodliness. Indeed, as Romans 3:7-8 makes clear and Romans 6:1 implies, Paul has been charged with this very thing.

Paul takes up this question, typically, not in terms of the individual believer in a one-on-one relationship with God, but at the very point where the Galatians are living as they used to, when the flesh held sway. Paul therefore warns the Galatians not to let their new freedom in Christ serve as a base of operations for the flesh (5:13), meaning in this case to continue to engage in strife within the community of faith (v. 15). Rather, in love they are to "perform the duties of a slave to one another" (v. 13). For love like this "fulfills the law" (v. 14).

Paul's response to vv. 13 and 15 is vv. 16-26. He begins in v. 16 with the basic imperative—and promise. "Walk in the Spirit," he urges them, "and you will not carry out the desire of the flesh." Since this responds to v. 15, he is not talking about the inner life of the believers, but of giving in to ungodly behavior within the community. After all, the works of the flesh that follow, all have to do with behavior, and eight of the fifteen items mentioned are sins of discord within the believing community.

Verse 17 functions to elaborate v. 16, and does so by way of what has been said in vv. 13-15. The elaboration simply says what we have seen him say elsewhere: walking in the Spirit is incompatible with life according to the flesh, because these two are in utter opposition to one another. And because they are utterly incompatible, those who live in the Spirit may not do whatever they please, that is, their new freedom in Christ does not permit them to continue living as they used to, by eating and devouring one another.

Thus the flesh-Spirit contrast has to do with those who have entered the new way of life brought about by Christ and the Spirit; Paul is urging them to live this way by the power of the Spirit. His point is that the Spirit stands in opposition to the other way of living, and is fully capable of empowering one to live so. It is not that Paul does not care about the inner life; he does indeed. But here he cares especially that the way God's people live provide a radical alternative to the world around them. Those who so walk by the Spirit will not keep on destroying the Christian community through strife and conflict.

In all the passages where Paul sets the Spirit against the flesh he insists that through the death of Christ and the gift of the Spirit, the flesh has been mortally wounded—killed, in his language. It is not possible, therefore, that from Paul's perspective a Spirit person would be living in such a way that she or he is sold as a slave to sin, who is unable to do the good she or he wants to do because of being held prisoner to the law of sin.

Believers live between the times. The already mortally wounded flesh will be finally brought to its end at the coming of Christ. The Spirit, already a present possession, will be fully realized at the same coming. To the degree that the old age has not yet passed away, we still must learn to walk by the Spirit, to behave in keeping with the Spirit, and to sow to the Spirit. We can do so precisely because the Spirit is sufficient. In Paul's view, we live in the flesh, only in the sense of living in the present body of humiliation, subject to the realities of the present age; but we do not walk according to the flesh. Such a way of life belongs to the past, and those who live that way are outside Christ and "shall not inherit the [final eschatological] kingdom of God" (Gal 5:21).

Paul is always a realist. The "new righteousness" that fulfills Torah, effected by the Spirit, is itself both already and not yet. To return to the preceding chapter, the coming of the Spirit means that "divine infection," not divine perfection, has set in. Our lives are now led by the one responsible for inspiring the law in the first place. But that does not mean that God's people cannot still be "overtaken in a fault" (Gal 6:1). The resolution of such between-the-times trespassing of God's righteous requirement is for the rest of God's Spirit people to restore such a one through the Spirit's gentleness. It means regularly to experience God's forgiveness and grace. It does *not* mean to accept constantly living in willful sin as inevitable, like a slow leak deflating our lives, as though the Spirit were not sufficient for life in the present.

———

If this explanation does not satisfy those of you who live in a constant struggle with some besetting sin, my word to you is to take heart from the gospel. I do not minimize the struggle. But you are loved by God, and that love has been "shed abroad in your heart by the Spirit." The key to life in the Spirit for some is to spend much more quiet time in thanksgiving and praise for what God has done—and is doing, and promises to do—and less time on introspection, focused on your failure to match up to the law.

Whenever you do feel like getting even for what someone has done to you rather than forgiving them as Christ has forgiven you, you are made to realize once more that you do still live between the times, between the time the infection set in and the perfection will be realized.... But by the Spirit's leading, neither do you do whatever you wish—tear into somebody for what they have done to you—as you used to do without thinking. The Spirit, God's own presence—his *empowering* presence—is within, and will lead you into appropriate responses.

Finally, to bring this discussion full circle, here is where your being a member of the body comes in. Since the ultimate goal of salvation is for us individually to belong as a growing, contributing, edifying member of the people of God, others in the body exist for the same purpose, and thus should serve you in the same way. Don't try to be a lone ranger Christian, slugging it out on your own. Seek out those in the community to whom you can be accountable and let them join you in your desire to grow into Christ's likeness.

"My greatest burden is to live with such openness and transparency that God's people see His glory and freedom expressed in who I am...as well as what I say." So states Dr. Harvey R. Brown, Jr. who left his administrative position at Asbury College in Wilmore, Kentucky, to found Impact Ministries, Inc.—a preaching and teaching ministry dedicated to the renewal of Christ's Church. A United Methodist clergyman, Dr. Brown has served as pastor, campus minister, college teacher and administrator, staff and parish development consultant, and chaplain in the United States Army. He is uniquely able to communicate with Christians over a broad spectrum of traditions and belief systems. His driving passion is to see the Church of Jesus Christ renewed; filled with the holiness of God's presence; empowered through the restoration of all the gifts, graces, and offices that the Holy Spirit bestows; and prepared to receive the coming end-time harvest.

Chapter 3*

Encountering the Power of Sanctification

by Dr. Harvey R. Brown, Jr.

The lights from the ceiling refracted into rainbow-like prisms as I opened my eyes. There I was, lying on the ballroom floor of the Regal Riverfront Hotel in St. Louis. Mixed feelings of relief and wonder rushed my emotions as I stared upward—the only way you can when you're flat on your back. Tears that were previously pouring from the corners of my eyes had puddled into my ears. Some now dripped onto the floor.

Trying to regain my focus, I sat up and looked around. As I wiped my face with my hands, I saw that only a handful of people remained in the room. *How long was I down?* I wondered, soon realizing that it didn't matter. What really mattered was the ever-increasing sense of the wonderful presence of my heavenly Father. All the earlier feelings of embarrassment and apprehension were now gone. I was aware of nothing but love—Father's love for me and my love for Him.

This must be it! This must be the power encounter everyone has been talking about, I thought. To see firsthand what people were calling renewal, I had come to the "Praying Down the Fire" conference that was sponsored

---

* Portions of this chapter are excerpted from Dr. Brown's book, *When God Strikes the Match: Igniting a Passion for Holiness and Renewal* (Shippensburg, PA: Revival Press, 1997).

by Randy Clark and the St. Louis Vineyard Christian Fellowship. My search had led me from the safe, predictable confines of a Christian college campus directly into a head-on encounter with the God of the universe!

I tried to stand up, but found my legs too wobbly. Sitting there on the floor—my arms wrapped around my knees, kind of hugging myself—I reflected with a sense of wonder on how God had brought me to this point. I could hardly believe how much my life had changed since I retired from the U.S. Army chaplaincy a year earlier to join the administration at Asbury College in Wilmore, Kentucky.

At Asbury I had discovered that the majority of the 1,200 young men and women in the student body were committed believers. Many had already been involved in short-term mission trips. Some were gifted musicians dedicating their talents to the glory of God. Most radiated a personal faith combined with an unbridled enthusiasm for the things of the Lord. I saw in these students an image that reflected the way I had been on the same campus 26 years earlier.

Watching these enthusiastic young believers brought me face-to-face with the fact that something had happened to that image of what I had been as an Asbury student. It had become significantly blurred by time...and by *sin*. The more I was with these marvelous young Christians, the more I realized that my interior world had become a desert wasteland. I was holding solid, biblically orthodox truth, but the life of the Spirit was a distant memory. Something had happened to my zeal for the Lord. The fire that had burned in my bones was now little more than embers. I was living and proclaiming a memory. There was no currency in my spirituality. I was barren, bereft of any real joy in Christ.

In some ways I had become a caricature of the churchmen—primarily preachers—I had turned to as a young believer. Trying to find someone who understood and identified with my newfound enthusiasm for the Savior, I went from leader to leader. What I frequently discovered was a *professional Christian*—someone paid to do church but who lacked passion and fire. Sometimes these leaders seemed to appreciate what was going on in my life, but I rarely sensed a resonance between us as I talked about my new birth or the discoveries I was finding in the Word. Over a period of time, without realizing it, I had migrated from the place of an enthusiastic believer to the position of a person more concerned about professional acceptance.

After college and graduate school, I had learned how to adapt to the "system." Being United Methodist, I am part of a denomination that is a theological mixed bag—you can find a full range of beliefs from fighting fundamentalists to flaming liberals. Clergy most frequently tilt toward the liberal view, while people in the pews tend to be more conservative in their beliefs. Yet no matter where you found yourself on the theological spectrum, if you wanted to succeed as a pastor, you learned how to fit in. Cookie-cutter clergy stood the best chance of thriving in the church. If you had fire, it was best to keep it in the fireplace and not let it spread. Don't walk near the margins or go too fast. Be mainstream and respectable, learn the ropes, don't ask too many questions, and certainly, don't rock the boat. Play by the rules and the system will take care of you.

Although I hadn't set out to let professionalism replace passion for ministry, I had gradually drifted toward the center of acceptability. I saw no developing conflict between being baptized by the system and doing effective ministry. After all, what better place was there to be responsive to the Lord than as a person of influence in a denomination with 8.5 million members?

Over the years, I had honed the mechanics of ministry to a sharp edge. I knew when to speak a word of comfort or just sit silently by, nodding my head in response to the people to whom I was listening. I carefully crafted my sermons to capture and hold attention, designing them to peak at just the right moment to achieve the desired effect. I took additional training to qualify as a staff and parish development consultant. I reveled in the fact that my peers recognized my effectiveness and that my superiors consistently lauded my preaching skill and ministry performance.

What had happened, however, was that I had substituted my own efforts, energies, and education for the leadership and presence of the Holy Spirit. Although these are not necessarily mutually exclusive, I fell into the trap Paul had described as "having a form of godliness, but denying the power thereof" (2 Tim. 3:5a KJV). Mine was a self-directed ministry. When comparing myself to other clergy, I found it fairly easy to be puffed up. Favorable statistics in terms of the number of people saved or touched by the Lord made me think that God's blessing was upon my ministry. I didn't factor that the Lord was honoring the proclamation of His Word, not necessarily the one who was proclaiming it. I was mistaking God's mercy for His favor.

There was another significant dynamic that was at work in my interior world. I wrestled with a recurring problem of lust and pornography that was pushed down and repressed, only to rear its ugly head sufficiently to make me feel that I was destined to lead a life of defeat and powerlessness over sin. The cyclical trap that Paul described in

Romans 7—wanting to do right and not being able—seemed to describe the internal hopelessness that I felt. Inwardly I longed for a deliverance that always seemed just out of reach. I had bargained and pleaded with God, promising Him that if He would take the compulsion away that I would never do it again, only to fall once again into a repetitive cycle of addictive behavior. I was trapped.

I felt a glimmer of hope when my chapel at Fort Monmouth, New Jersey, hosted Don Francisco, a Christian balladeer, in a concert. During an interlude between songs, he referred to how the Lord Jesus had delivered him from addiction to pornography. I wanted so much to talk with him afterward, or even to call him on the phone and ask him to pray for me. However, the shame of my sinfulness kept me from bringing it to the light. I wanted God to deal with me privately so that no one else would have to know. I was someone important in the church, at least in my own eyes, and I should be above and beyond such behavior. I would just have to work this out on my own.

I managed to make an uneasy peace with the monster within—refusing it when I could and giving in when I couldn't stand it any longer, hoping God would forgive me one more time. I wished I could take back the territory the monster had claimed. I longed for a holiness of life where I would not always be battling a besetting sin. But I didn't want a kind of piety that I had seen in some holiness circles where people seemed to be tied up in "not's" (it's *not* right to do this...*not* right to do that). I longed for a holiness that wasn't based on striving. I wanted to be *really* free, but held out little hope that anything would ever be fundamentally different in my life until I got to Heaven.

It was ironic that, after 23 years as a pastor and a chaplain, I was welcomed back to Asbury College as a senior leader in a holiness school when I had never proclaimed the doctrine of sanctification as I'd been taught at Asbury. I couldn't. I didn't see it at work in my own life. Oh, I had tried. But regardless of all my attempts at holy living, I secretly saw my life as a dismal failure.

On campus I became acquainted with people who seemed to have the freedom I coveted. The students were always talking about what Jesus was doing in their lives. Many had fantastic testimonies of God's grace and deliverance. Some had experienced trauma and brokenness beyond my comprehension, yet the Lord had rescued them and set them free. Others were living lives completely liberated from past compulsions and addictions. Listening to these students talk about their love for Jesus, I sensed a softening in my heart. It was as if a window had opened ever so slightly, bringing in a refreshing breeze. Deep within me a stirring was beginning.

At the same time, I kept hearing about winds of renewal moving across the face of the Church. It had come through Wilmore six months before we moved back into the community. A local church had been the scene of a conference entitled "Light the Fire"—and folks in Wilmore had been touched by it. As a result, a number of my new friends spoke frequently, and with great energy, about the *current move of God*. I felt, however, that I had to see it myself rather than just accept someone else's opinion. That's why I'd gone to the "Praying Down the Fire" conference in St. Louis.

When I arrived in St. Louis I explicitly told the Lord that I was not seeking a special experience. My only goal was to genuinely know Him better and love Him more. If I were to have an "experience," that was okay. But if I were to return home without experiencing any phenomenon or manifestation, yet loved Christ more, it would be worth the trip and the expense. I felt that I was being totally honest with God about what I expected. Others' opinions and descriptions were no longer sufficient. I had to see for myself.

My first glimpse of renewal came when Randy Clark spoke to over 100 pastors in a pre-conference meeting at the hotel. "The renewal coming to the Church is like waves breaking upon the seashore," he said. "It is not a single splash, but a series of visitations by the Holy Spirit to accomplish what God wants to do in these days."

Randy went on to describe the outpouring in Toronto as a first wave of renewal to refresh a dry Church. He saw successive waves coming to equip the Church to minister salvation to the nations—to equip the Church to take the message of God's love to the ends of the earth.

His words rang a bell in my heart. My concern for the lost was as high as it had ever been. In fact, a week before leaving for St. Louis, I had been involved in the nitty-gritty of one-on-one prison evangelism at the Kentucky State Reformatory and had been moved with a renewed compassion for those who do not know the Savior. Here was one of the key leaders of renewal saying things that were resonating with everything I had recently been feeling.

Randy Clark has the heart of an evangelist, I thought. *He's not a feel-good, get-a-religious-buzz preacher. These people are talking Kingdom talk. This is no "just-bless-me" club. They have a real passion for the lost!*

During the final moments of the pastors' meeting, the Lord really got my attention. Fred Grewe, an associate of Randy Clark's, came to the front during a chorus after Randy's prayer for the lost. He took the microphone and said, "The Lord has shown me that there are pastors here who are continually struggling with pornography and masturbation. If you want to be free—to be released from this—I invite you to come to the back of the room for prayer."

My mind began to spin. *Could it be that the Lord is finally going to set me free?* I wondered. *No, this word is probably for others.* After all, I had shed tears on altar rails on three continents, begging God for deliverance. But no matter how many times I had prayed, I always slipped back into old patterns of destructive behavior.

Why would prayer now do any good? Why expose my sin in front of all these pastors? What would my colleagues at Asbury College say if they were to find out? I'd better just deal with this on my own.

Then I glanced back over my shoulder and saw that a number of men were already at the back of the room. *If I don't hurry, there's not going to be any room left for me,* I thought. Something—or Someone—seemed to be calling me to respond.

I eased away from my front-row seat and turned toward the side aisle, hoping no one would notice me. However, my ears were so hot that I was sure their redness would attract attention to me like a jet fighter attracts a heat-seeking missile. But as I made my way to the back of the room, I discovered that every eye was not focused on me. Most of the people had their heads bowed and eyes closed. Obviously, they were interceding for the work Father was doing in that room.

I was last in the line of the men who responded to Fred's invitation. After I stood there a few minutes, Fred came to pray for me. For a brief time he just stood there looking at me intently. I felt as if he were peering directly into my heart.

"You have been unable to fulfill the exceedingly high expectations in your life," Fred finally said, "and you are retreating into a fantasy world for relief and solace."

Wham! His words had nailed me right between the eyes. Although I'd never thought of my problems in this way, I knew that God had read my mail. God knew *me*! And, this was it! My temperament is the most self-critical of the 16 types described by the Myers-Briggs Personality Type Inventory. By the time these thoughts had gone through my mind, Fred was gently placing his hands on my head. As he took authority over the problem in my life, I felt the power. Someone eased me to the floor, and I slipped quietly into a peaceful state of rest. Waves of mercy began washing over me. I knew a miraculous healing was taking place.

While I was on the floor, the Lord reminded me of the time when, as a 12-year-old on a class trip to Washington, D.C., my friend Pete had introduced me to masturbation. After this, the practice had become a regular escape from loneliness and unfulfilled expectations in my life. All these years I had struggled to overcome the habit; now God was dealing a deathblow to the root of the problem by going back to the source. No longer would I be dealing with the symptoms. I was going to free—really free!

Yet there was more. The Lord also reminded me of the issue of pornography as a supporting actor in this lurid drama. Eight years earlier, while away from home for a nine-week Army training course, I had rented an X-rated video. "I'm just curious," I had told myself. "What real harm can come from this? I'm away from home in another state where no one knows me. I'll only do this once to satisfy my curiosity, and that will be it."

How wrong I was! The images replayed over and over in my mind until they became a stronghold in my life. Now I had opened a door and was confronting another enemy that I would have to battle repeatedly. I had allowed the enemy a beachhead in my life, and he, as the *accuser*, frequently exploited me by dispatching raiding parties to keep me harassed, distracted, and confused.

I might defeat one assault only to find devilish snipers shooting at me again. These allied enemies of masturbation and pornography carried on guerrilla warfare within me, managing to win enough skirmishes to make me feel that I could never really win the war. Only occasional lulls in the battle allowed me any kind of uneasy rest. But I always knew there could be another ambush around the next corner.

This internal warfare—with its steady stream of struggles—tainted any Kingdom victories I experienced. Sure, God was using my preaching to change peoples' lives, but the sinful failures in my private world kept plaguing me with guilt and condemnation—real guilt and real condemnation—that gnawed at me like hungry vultures devouring roadkill. But, it all ended that night on the floor in St. Louis when God overwhelmed me with His love. The vultures were vanquished. The Victor had come.

In my time of reflection there on the floor of the hotel ballroom, I thought of an athletic contest as the best description of what had been going on in my life. I had been wrestling with the Lord. Suddenly, He had changed the rules and went to no-holds-barred, promptly pinning me to the mat with His love. Then, He lifted me up and raised my hands, declaring me the victor. Glory to His marvelous name!

What made the difference between that night in St. Louis and all the other occasions I sought freedom from my spiritual bondage? Having asked myself this question many times, I think I may have discovered some answers.

Over the course of my Christian life I had, with varying degrees of intensity, quested for righteousness. I had pursued holiness; but, finding it illusive, I had abandoned the quest in disillusionment. All I'd discovered were unfulfilled hopes of holiness. I felt like someone consigned to watching previews when they had been promised a whole movie.

My struggles, I now know, were much deeper than wrestling with the acts of sin I committed. At the root of these sinful behaviors was something fundamentally flawed. My sins were the evidence of the brokenness of character that Christians refer to as the *carnal* or *sin nature*. This genetic predisposition to sin was the controlling factor in my life. No matter how hard I tried to overcome the behaviors, I was no more able to change them than a leopard is able to change its spots. My sins were the evidence of my nature. It was more than my *behavior* that needed to be changed. *I* was the problem. There was nothing *I* could do about it. Yet coming to grips with this reality was a severe mercy.

Had I been able to overcome on my own, it would have been a work of the flesh—whether by self-reform, behavior modification, or strength of will—and works of the flesh are wholly inadequate to deal with root issues that are spiritual. I had exhausted every remedy for my sinful behavior, yet I had remained stuck in a defeated life. The root of the behavior—my sin nature—needed to be dealt with before I could be delivered from the dichotomous existence in which I was trapped.

I believed—at least on an intellectual level—that the power of God was fully sufficient to deliver a person from the bondage of sin. However, because of my consistent failures, I never expected to see this deliverance actualized in my own life. Accordingly, I could never proclaim through my preaching the full freedom of a sanctified life. Although I steadfastly declared free salvation for all men, my failures meant that I could not with integrity deliver the full gospel of salvation with complete victory over sin.

I knew that Zacharias prophesied about the sanctifying and keeping work of the coming Christ at the birth of John the Baptist. In the first words he spoke after recovering his voice, he said that the Messiah would "rescue us from the hand of our enemies" and "enable us to serve Him without fear in holiness and righteousness before Him all our days" (Lk. 1:74-75). Before my St. Louis experience, however, I had never been able to proclaim the validity of this prophecy.

In the current vernacular, "power encounter" is used to describe an occasion where God profoundly touches someone at a personal level through the operation of spiritual gifts or some other manifestation of the presence of the Holy Spirit. My encounter with the overwhelming power of God in St. Louis was the entry point through which I experienced the irresistible, cleansing, sanctifying power of our Christ—a power strong enough to deal with the root issue of sin in my life.

Because Fred Grewe was willing to listen to the Holy Spirit's revelation that there were pastors struggling with sins of pornography and masturbation, I was set free to serve the Lord "in holiness and righteousness." God spoke to my heart through Fred's step of faith to share the Spirit-inspired revelation that he had received.

God spoke to me again through Fred's prayer for me. He articulated something so specific and so personal that I knew Fred could have said it only because of a gift of the Holy Spirit operating through him. I cannot describe the impact of this spoken revelation. Because of it, I *knew* beyond *any* doubt that my heavenly Father was dealing with me as an individual. I wasn't just another warm body standing among a group of sexually hung-up pastors. I knew—really knew—that I was going to be set free. Why else would He have demonstrated His power so conclusively through all this revelation? Why else would the presence of God so overwhelm me that I could no longer stand?

The power was a prelude to the promise. I collapsed to the floor, overcome by the power of the Spirit of God. I rested in the Spirit as cleansing waves of love washed over me. I came up a changed man.

In his famous sermon "The Changed Life," Henry Drummond said that every verb in the New Testament relating to change is in the passive voice. That means that change is something God does, not something we do. The nature of true spiritual change is that we, through our own efforts, cannot effect real change, cannot effect anything of eternal value. What we cannot do for ourselves, the Lord does for us. In St. Louis, He did something for me that I had been trying for decades to do for myself. As I found myself in Him, my sin life was subsumed by His righteousness. When I arose from the hotel floor, the essence of who I am had been mysteriously changed by an encounter with the power of God.

Am I saying I will never sin? Absolutely not! What I am saying is that God moved me into a position in Christ where, through His resurrection power, I have the potential for living above habitual sin. In addition to freeing us from the guilt and penalty of sin, our Lord, through His Holy

Spirit, sanctifies us. He declares us to be holy and causes us to share in His divine nature wherein we are being changed "from glory to glory."

As Paul says in Second Corinthians 3:17-18:

Now the Lord is the Spirit, and where the Spirit of the Lord is, there is freedom. And we, who with unveiled faces all reflect the Lord's glory, are being transformed into His likeness with ever-increasing glory, which comes from the Lord, who is the Spirit.

Think of that! We are being conformed (shaped, fashioned) into the image of God's Son. Again, as Paul says:

For those God foreknew He also predestined to be conformed to the likeness of His Son, that He might be the firstborn among many brothers (Romans 8:29).

Some believers insist that we must sin. I thank God, through Jesus Christ my Lord, that I now know through experience—as well as study—that the Lord is "able to keep that which I have committed unto Him against that day" (2 Tim. 1:12 KJV). Because we are in Christ and have the Holy Spirit's empowering presence, *we do not have to sin.*

Consider Jude 24-25 (KJV):

Now unto Him that is able to keep you from falling, and to present you faultless before the presence of His glory with exceeding joy, to the only wise God our Saviour, be glory and majesty, dominion and power, both now and ever. Amen.

Jesus is able to keep us from falling—right here, right now. We don't have to fall. We don't have to stumble. We don't have to sin. Our Christ is big enough, strong enough, and holy enough to keep us. His work is sufficient and complete. Because the divine nature of Christ is imparted to us through His Holy Spirit, the Lord is not relegated to a posture of having to wait patiently for us to come to Heaven so that we will no longer practice sin.

The sanctification imparted to us expresses itself in joy. In addition to being kept from falling back into old sinful habits, I now fully experience the joy of the Lord, "exceeding great joy." In the presence of His glory, there is "righteousness, and peace, and joy" (Rom. 14:17 KJV). As a sanctified believer, I walk in the glorious liberty—joyful liberty—of the children of God. The Lord has taken back *my land!*

Call it a *power encounter.* Call it *sanctification.* Call it *deliverance.* Call it a *miracle.* Call it what you will. By any name, I call it **freedom in Christ**.

Section II

Taking the Message to the Street

Michael L. Brown (Ph.D., New York University) is President of the Brownsville Revival School of Ministry. With a heart to see Jesus glorified in the earth, he has carried the message of repentance and revival throughout America and to numerous foreign countries. His books have been translated into more than a dozen languages, and his scholarly work in Old Testament and Hebrew studies has been published in leading journals and encyclopedias. It is his desire to wake up the sleeping Church and to see his people Israel saved.

Chapter 4

True and False Conversion

by Dr. Michael L. Brown

It was the revival scholar James Edwin Orr who made the concise but cutting comment, "The only proof of the new birth is the new life." How could it be otherwise? Something *really happens* when a person has an encounter with the living God; when he or she is set free from slavery to sin, delivered from the dominion of darkness and transferred into the Kingdom of light, liberated from bondage to Satan, and made into a child of God; is washed in the blood of the Lamb, indwelt by the Holy Spirit, and born from above into a whole new life. Being "saved" is more than just a figure of speech or a theological construct!

In fact, it can be argued that the ultimate "power encounter" between God and man is not divine healing, the baptism in the Spirit, the exorcism of demons, or the reception of a prophetic message, but rather the experience of conversion. Yes, the *experience* of conversion— and I fully mean to emphasize that word.

Then why, it might be asked, do so many converts bear so few marks of conversion? Why do so many *saints* seem so unsaintly? Or, to put it another way, why do our churches seem to be filled with what I have (sarcastically and somewhat imprecisely) called the "semi-saved"? According to Orr, this too is easily explained: It is primarily the result of spiritual "birth defects." In other words, these woefully shallow, hardly committed, almost always lukewarm believers—"saved" though they may be—are the product of a defective gospel message. And so, because our gospel message has been defective, our disciples are now defective and the American "born-again" Church is defective as well. This is a vicious cycle of "genetically" flawed reproduction with far-reaching consequences.

Shortly before his death in 1987, Orr wrote these words:

"Defective evangelism has become a national scandal. While evangelistic enterprises are claiming untold numbers of converts, a national poll announcing that multi-millions claim to be 'born-again,' yet a national newspaper notes that the 'so-called evangelical awakening' seems to have had no effect upon the morals of the nation, while murder, robbery, rape, prostitution, pornography and the other social evils are abounding."[1]

Writing in 1985, Carl F.H. Henry made a similar observation:

"Speaking for a national morality movement, an evangelical leader recently remarked: 'The United States has turned away from God. It mocks God. It worships a twentieth century Baal...incarnated in sensuality, material goods, and immorality of every kind'...Yet only a few years ago we were told that a new evangelical awakening had dawned in America; this very decade, it was said, is the decade of the evangelicals."[2]

What is a major cause of this spiritual and moral crisis? Spiritual birth defects! Millions of born-again Christians today are in pathetic spiritual shape because they were not properly birthed into the Kingdom. They did not understand what they were being *saved from* and what they were being *saved to*.

Here are some questions worth considering: At the point of conversion—or at some point shortly thereafter—did these people recognize their desperate need for a Savior and so flee for refuge into His arms, leaving the world behind? Or was Jesus merely a means to an end for them, a solution to a present problem? Did they understand their guilt before a holy God and so give themselves to Him without reserve when He pronounced them pardoned and free, or did they somehow think that they

---

1.   J. Edwin Orr, *My All, His All* (Wheaton, IL: International Awakening Press, 1989), 7-8.

2.   Cited in Michael L. Brown, *It's Time to Rock the Boat: A Call to God's People to Rise Up and Preach a Confrontational Gospel* (Shippensburg, PA: Destiny Image, 1993), 40.

did God (or the church) a favor by "joining"? Did they have any idea that the Master Himself was quite specific in His entry-level requirements for all prospective followers, or did they imagine that it was one thing to be forgiven and quite another to be one of those "really radical" or "holy" Christians? What kind of gospel message did these people hear when they came to the Lord?

The British Bible teacher David Pawson suggests that the first question an altar worker should ask someone responding to a call for salvation is, "What are you asking Jesus to save you from?" *That* would certainly open things up! And it would also expose the lack of clarity in our gospel presentation. What *are* we saying to those who don't know the Lord? This should give us pause for serious thought. In fact, we would do well to wonder what would happen if, in our preaching, we simply quoted the words of the Lord Jesus in the Gospels when He made it clear that following Him required total allegiance and a complete change of life. This would certainly rock some boats! (It would certainly upset the devil!)

Being a *disciple* of Jesus (and that is what the believers were called in Acts) is a radical thing. After all, if I was traveling South and Jesus was traveling North, wouldn't the call to follow Him require an about-face on my part? His call is no less radical in the spiritual realm! Jesus demanded that all those who wanted to follow Him deny themselves, take up their cross, forsake all, no longer serve any other masters, walk the straight and narrow way, and love no one and nothing more than Him (see, e.g., Mt. 6:24; 16:24-26; Lk. 13:22-30; 14:25-33; Jn. 12:24-25). Otherwise, Jesus made it plain that we have no business claiming allegiance to Him. To put it in clear, contemporary terms, He was saying, "If you won't take up your cross, don't even think about being My disciple!" Oh, that all of us started with this foundation! The spiritual condition of our churches today would be *very* different.

Just think of a young woman getting married without knowing that this act of holy union meant a lifetime commitment. Just think of a soldier joining the army without knowing that he would be called to fight in battle. Just think of a boxer entering the ring without knowing that his opponent would be trying to hit him too. All these images are preposterous and ridiculous, yet many of us have no problem thinking of someone being "born again" without knowing that following Jesus means death to sin and self-rule, without knowing that the Savior who redeems them must be the Lord who rules them, and without knowing that they are saved to serve.

Unfortunately, we have departed so far from the biblical message of the gospel that some readers actually *struggle* with statements like those just made, as if they were guilty of mixing grace with works or justification with legalism. What a lack of understanding of scriptural truth this demonstrates. Salvation *transforms* sinners into saints. In other words, Jesus is a Savior who really saves!

That's why Paul could declare so emphatically, "I am not ashamed of the gospel, because it is the power of God for the salvation of everyone who believes: first for the Jew, then for the Gentile" (Rom. 1:16). Chew on those words for a moment: The gospel is "the power of God for the salvation of everyone who believes." That is to say, the gospel is not only the legal means by which God pronounces guilty sinners to be righteous through faith in the blood of Jesus; the gospel is the *power to save them* as well, which means to save them from sin and the dominion of darkness. Otherwise, it is no salvation at all. But if we preach a gospel message without power, we will have converts without power. In God's Kingdom, everything produces after its own kind.

What then are some of the symptoms of Christians with spiritual birth defects? Here are a few:

1) Such believers will have low standards of holiness and little conviction of sinful habits and actions. Why? Because the standards of God were not presented to them when they came to the Lord. Instead, He was simply there to relieve them of their guilt or help them through their problems, and so, they were never confronted with the all-exposing mirror of the Word.

2) Such believers will find concepts such as sacrifice and suffering for the Lord to be completely foreign. Why? Because they never recognized how much mercy God had on them in their lost estate, and consequently, they have no idea how indebted to the Lord they now are. Their sense of gratitude is skin-deep (at best), since they neither realize the price that was paid for their souls nor the depth to which they did *not* deserve such payment.

3) Such believers will have little burden to share their faith with the lost. Why? First, because their change of life was relatively minor, so they don't have that much to share with others. Second, because preaching the gospel often means embarrassment and rejection, they feel that it simply costs too much to witness. It's easier for them to keep their "Christianity" to themselves. And as for everyone else, their motto is, "Live and let live!"

4) Such believers will hop from church to church when pressure is applied to their lives. Why? Because Christianity for them means an improved and even "convenient" lifestyle. So when things get rough, rather than grow in grace and persevere, they will go where things are easier. Of course, because they have some "gospel" foundation, most of them don't abandon the faith entirely. But because they came to the Lord to make their lives "better" (meaning, for them, *easier* as opposed to *holier*), they surely won't stay around when things get tough. They'll just find another group that doesn't challenge them!

It all boils down to this: For years we have preached a cheap gospel and peddled a soft Savior, and now we are paying the price. We have effectively denied the transforming power of the gospel! No wonder so many believers find themselves barely keeping their heads above the flood tide of sin, barely looking and acting different than the world, barely shining the light. For these dear, spiritually deprived people, the whole goal of their walk with God is to avoid backsliding another day. That is not the expected, New Testament norm! The blood of Jesus, the indwelling Holy Spirit, the keeping power of the Father, and the living Word of God are far more powerful than that. Aren't they?

Of course, I recognize that all of us have struggles and temptations, that all of us have dry seasons and trying times, and that even some of those converted in the midst of powerful spiritual outpourings can still fall away or become lukewarm. But the "defection" rate among those who have been soundly converted and scripturally discipled is absolutely minimal in comparison, and, perhaps more importantly, the fruit-bearing, Christ-glorifying, Kingdom-advancing works of these believers *far* outstrip the meager labors of their defectively born-again brothers and sisters.

In my 1990 book, *How Saved Are We?*, I gave this challenge:

"*It's time for some serious soul searching.* What kind of 'born again' experience have we had if it calls for almost no personal sacrifice, produces virtually no separation from the world, and breeds practically no hatred of sin? Where is the evidence of our 'new nature'?

"Something is wrong with our 'salvation' experience! *Bad fruits mean bad roots....*

"Our gospel message has been doubly defective. We have injured our hearers in two ways: We have failed to tell them the old life must end; and we have failed to show them new life in Him."[3]

These words were followed up in 1991 with a related challenge in my subsequent book, *Whatever Happened to the Power of God?* There I stated:

"We know very little about the gospel today. We share our testimonies with our friends and co-workers. We get people to pray the sinner's prayer and then we bring them to our discipleship classes. But so many times we fail to see real conversion, deep transformation, and genuine *salvation*....

"Because our preaching lacks punch, because we have not opened the eyes of the sinner to his lost state, because we hardly confront him with the reality of the living God, we have to lean on human techniques as well as a watered-down message. 'You don't have to *do* anything,' we say. 'Simply pray this little prayer—and whether you feel the witness in your heart or not, whether your life changes or not, whether you ever repent of your sin or not—it's done! Isn't that easy?' "[4]

The good news is that in the past ten years many other ministers have also rejected this skin-deep salvation message and are once again preaching the gospel in power (here in America too!). Consequently, many sinners are being radically converted (this has been a wonderful sight virtually every night in the Brownsville Revival—the revival in the Brownsville Assembly of God in Pensacola, Florida—for almost four years now, and it is happening in other places around the country too), and we are beginning to recover the reality of the glorious power of the death and resurrection of the Messiah. Glory and praise be to God! The same Spirit that raised Jesus from the dead raises us from the dead at the point of our conversion. We really pass from death to life.

Just consider Paul's words to the Corinthians:

Do you not know that the wicked will not inherit the kingdom of God? Do not be deceived: Neither the sexually immoral nor idolaters nor adulterers nor male prostitutes nor homosexual offenders nor

---

3.   Michael L. Brown, *How Saved Are We?* (Shippensburg, PA: Destiny Image Publishers, 1990), 2, 15.

4.   Michael L. Brown, *Whatever Happened to the Power of God?* (Shippensburg, PA: Destiny Image Publishers, 1991), 3, 42-43.

thieves nor the greedy nor drunkards nor slanderers nor swindlers will inherit the kingdom of God. And that is what some of you were. But you were washed, you were sanctified, you were justified in the name of the Lord Jesus Christ and by the Spirit of our God (1 Corinthians 6:9-11).

In this passage, Paul is declaring: "Corinthian believers, you *were* slaves to all kinds of sins and passions, but you have been: 1) washed; 2) sanctified; and 3) justified in the name of Jesus and by the Spirit's power."

How interesting it is that Paul doesn't give a precise "theological" order here—we might have expected him to have put "justified" first—but rather he gives an inclusive picture of what happened to these Corinthians when they were born again. Being pronounced "not guilty" is of no use at all if I continue to live in willful rebellion against my Maker. If I live a criminal life (being "wicked" in Paul's words just quoted above), then I will not inherit the Kingdom of God. The fact that I am "right with God" means that I am in right legal standing with Him *and* that I now live righteously before Him. That's the power of the gospel! The proof of its lasting power at Corinth was seen in the fact that the Corinthians were quick to repent and pursue God's holiness when rebuked by Paul (see 2 Cor. 7:8-11).

More than 300 years ago, John Bunyan wrote a quaint but poignant poem about his own spiritual pilgrimage, and its message remains relevant today. For wherever you are spiritually, even if, upon reflection, you may now consider yourself to be the product of a "defective" gospel, the poem brings good news: There is still time to change and make a fresh new start, provided that you are ready to sprint! And for those of you who are declaring the gospel to the lost, the poem is a reminder of the importance of our new "beginnings" in Jesus.

I leave you with Bunyan's words:

> Blessed be the day that I began
> A pilgrim for to be;
> And blessed also be that man
> That hereto moved me.

> 'Tis true, 'twas long ere I began
> To seek to live forever.
> But now I run fast as I can;
> 'Tis better late than never.

Our tears to joy, our fears to faith
Are turned, as we see.
Thus our beginning (as some saith),
Shows what our end will be.[5]

---

5.   Cited in Lewis A. Drummond, *Spurgeon: Prince of Preachers* (Grand Rapids: Kregel, 1992), 6.

Randy Clark is the senior pastor of the Vineyard Christian Fellowship of St. Louis, Missouri. Randy and his ministry, Global Awakening, are committed to the development of citywide leadership teams throughout the world. They have trained over 25,000 leaders and lay people in ministry team techniques for power evangelism, healing, and deliverance in the United States, Canada, England, Russia, Australia, and Latin America. Randy's passion is to see people saved, healed, delivered, and helped according to Luke 4:18. "I love to equip people to pray for the sick. I love to see burned-out pastors set on fire for God and empowered to minister in greater anointing," he says. It is his desire to see the Church continue the power ministry of Jesus in the earth today.

Chapter 5

Power Evangelism to Reach the Lost

by Randy Clark

Power Evangelism to Reach the Lost

1921. St. Louis, Missouri.

> After that the sergeant of police assigned regular details, changed twice a day, to keep people from being trampled or crushed against the temple, where thousands were unable to gain admission. People shut out the day before would begin gathering at the doors at five in the morning. By nine o'clock the streets would begin to fill; at 12:15 the police would open the doors, and in five minutes the house would be packed. Police estimated that on several occasions 4,000 or 5,000 were turned away. [The temple's capacity was 3,000.] ...people would stand outside the temple through an entire service. They would cling to a brick corner or ledge, in the hope that just touching the building in which God worked so powerfully must be a blessing.... At the end of two weeks, when the party had outgrown Moolah Temple, an ad hoc committee of ministers raised $1,500 to rent the 12,000-seat St. Louis Coliseum (with standing room for 4,000 more) for the last week.... Any

promoter can tell you how difficult it is to fill a hall that size today, for only one night, with or without an admission charge. Only pop stars can do it, and a few political personalities; and they require elaborate advance publicity. Before rock'n'roll only an act like Mary Garden, the soprano, or Harry Houdini would book the St. Louis Coliseum for several nights—and neither star would have risked this without several weeks of advance drumming.

Upon thirty-six hours' notice Aimee transferred her meeting to the coliseum. The next day it was full, and for the rest of the week Aimee preached three times daily to overflow crowds of 16,000 so that the police were again called to keep people from being crushed against the doors."[1]

The famous Aimee Semple McPherson meetings described above were held the last week of April 1921. What drew the crowds? Power evangelism.

1954. Buenos Aires, Argentina.

The Atlantic stadium with a seating capacity of twenty-five thousand was rented. God began to stretch out His hand, even though the beginning crowds were small. The news spread rapidly; God began to heal. Before long, larger crowds were coming out to see and hear this 'miracle worker' as he was called. Ushers were soon working 12-hour-a-day shifts. Often the bleachers were occupied several hours before the services were scheduled to begin. Because of the many people who had to remain on the outside, loudspeakers were installed. Inside the stadium, the walk-ways were filled, then the crowd pushed down the fence surrounding the playing field and surged across, filling the field as well. They pushed down the doors of the stadium and shoved their way in.

...Because of the overflow crowds, a much larger stadium was rented—the great Huracan stadium, the largest in the country with capacity for 180,000. It had never been filled; no sports event or political rally had ever filled it. And now the little, unknown gospel preacher had dared to rent it. [An angel] had said that the wave of blessing God would send would fill the

1.   Daniel Mark Epstein, *Sister Aimee: The Life of Aimee Semple McPherson* (New York: Harcourt Brace & Company, 1993), 212-14.

largest places with vast multitudes seeking to hear the Gospel; rulers would hear the message. Now it was literally coming to pass.

...Outstanding healings took place, too numerous to recount.... Stolid cynicism gave way to hope. Proud Argentines became as emotional as any Pentecostal.... The lame were walking, the paralyzed set free. The blind were seeing, stretcher cases healed. Ambulances brought invalid patients and returned empty. Life and health flowed like a river, for God had come to Argentina.... An English paper of Buenos Aires reported one of the services favorably, estimating the crowds as being 200,000. It spoke of hundreds who waited from early morning for the stadium gates to open."[2]

This time the year was 1954, and the evangelist was American Tommy Hicks. Once again, it was power evangelism that drew the people.

Ironically, the pastors who organized the event originally believed that renting a venue to hold 1,500 would have been large enough. Argentina, prior to this outpouring of healing, had been resistant to the gospel as presented by Protestants. After more than 100 years of missionary work, very little headway had been made by the Protestant churches.[3]

McPherson and Hicks are merely two examples of the numerous healing evangelists throughout the twentieth century who successfully used a form of power evangelism. In 1977, Reinhard Bonnke had 40,000 people attend the last night of a crusade in Africa. Just a few days earlier, only a few hundred had been in attendance. What had drawn the others? It was the report of Jesus' healing ministry still at work today through the evangelist. Later, Bonnke saw much larger crowds at Ibadan, Nigeria. The crowd there was estimated at 500,000 by the press, but a more conservative estimate by Reinhard's team placed the numbers at about 250,000.

---

2.   Dr. R. Edward Miller, *Cry for Me Argentina: Revival Begins in City Bell* (Essex, England: Sharon Publications Ltd., 1988), 42, 43, 45.

3.   This healing crusade would change the atmosphere of Argentina and prepare the way for other healing evangelists such as Omar Cabrera Sr. and Carlos Annacondia. This is the opinion of Dr. Pablo Deiros, a leading scholar of Latin America and the leading scholar on the history of the Protestant church in Argentina. (Personal interview, 1998.)

In 1984, Carlos Annacondia saw 83,000 people make a decision to follow Christ in response to his gospel invitations in Mar del Plata, Argentina. Earlier that year he had seen another 50,000 decisions in La Plata. In 1985 he had two meetings where 60,200 and 57,000 respectively were saved. What drew so many people to Christ? The most distinctive aspect of an Annacondia crusade is the ministry of deliverance after the people accept Jesus. As soon as the people's names are taken of those who have responded to the altar call, Annacondia begins to come against demonic spirits in the people. Demons begin to manifest and the people are taken to a deliverance tent. Other aspects of his ministry include healing, people being slain in the Spirit, and teeth being filled with gold and platinum.[4] God used this phenomena to catch the interest of the press, who then called attention to Annacondia's crusades. Some of the crowds at these crusades have exceeded 100,000.[5]

Whether it was Aimee Semple McPherson in 1921, Tommy Hicks in 1954, Reinhard Bonnke in 1977, or Carlos Annacondia in 1987, one thing remains the same—people are drawn to Jesus when they see His healing power. It is also true that the miraculous healing ministry was a primary reason for the success of the missionary activities of those who believed and practiced it. This has been described by one scholar in the following way:

> "This burst of independent mission work—remarkably vital in contrast to the sluggish and impoverished mission programs of most denominations—resulted in stunning growth for worldwide Pentecostalism. The success of miracle-based evangelism seemed to Pentecostal leaders one more confirmation that God was behind the revival."[6]

Many more stories of men and women and their great evangelistic harvests could be listed, for there have been many such events witnessed throughout recent Church history. The most exciting aspect of power evangelism, however, isn't in the stories of the past; it is that which is yet to come. I believe the greatest healing move of God is in our near future. Many great men and women of God have prophesied that there will be

---

4.   While in Argentina, I was told that at one point you had to have at least four teeth supernaturally filled to even give a testimony because so many teeth had been filled.

5.   For more on Annacondia's ministry, see his book, *Listen to Me, Satan: Exercising Authority Over the Devil in Jesus' Name* (Orlando, FL: Creation House, 1998).

6.   David Harrell, Jr., *All Things Are Possible: The Healing and Charismatic Revivals in Modern America* (Bloomington, IN: Indiana University Press, 1975), 94.

a great revival at the end of time. I want to be a part of it, and I hope you do too.

Different Forms, One Goal

Evangelism is a priority for most of the Church. However, it is understood differently by different types of churches, all of whom have the same goal: to reach those without Jesus Christ. Within the last several years, the Holy Spirit has been inspiring and anointing numerous unique ways of reaching the lost. These methods vary from "prayer evangelism"[7] to "servant evangelism"[8] to the staggering international success of the Alpha program.[9]

Historically, "presence evangelism" and "presentation evangelism" have been two of the most frequently used methods. Presence evangelism emphasizes being salt and light in the world and society around us. It seeks to bring the love of God into hurting contexts, represented by orphanages, hospitals, relief efforts, and many other similar kinds of activity. Presentation evangelism, on the other hand, emphasizes sharing the gospel by presenting the claims of Christ and calling for a commitment to Christ. This form of evangelism is based more upon reason and logic and has an apologetic heavily dependent on reason to come to faith. Both of these forms have been used quite successfully to share the gospel.

---

7.   Popularized by Ed Silvoso, prayer evangelism is based on Luke 10:3-9 where Jesus tells us to do four things: to bless the lost (v. 5), to fellowship with them (v. 7), to meet their felt needs (v. 9), and to proclaim the gospel (v. 9). According to Silvoso, prayer evangelism is essentially "talking with God about our neighbors before we talk with our neighbors about God." For more on the power of prayer evangelism, read Silvoso's book, *That None Should Perish: How to Reach Entire Cities for Christ Through Prayer Evangelism* (Ventura, CA: Regal, 1994).

8.   Servant evangelism is based on the concept of serving people with deeds of kindness—such as free cold drinks on a hot day or free car washes with no strings attached—and thereby creating an environment to share the gospel. For more information on servant evangelism, read Steve Sjogren's book, *Conspiracy of Kindness: A Refreshing New Approach to Sharing the Love of Jesus with Others* (Ann Arbor, MI: Vine Books, 1993).

9.   Inspired by Nicky Gumbel, a rector on staff at Holy Trinity Brompton Anglican Church in London, Alpha is a practical introduction to the Christian faith presented in an informal setting. All attendees are allowed (and encouraged) to ask whatever question they choose. The practical topics include, "Who is Jesus," "Why did He die," "Why and how should I pray," "How God guides us," and "How does He heal." Participants learn about the Holy Spirit during a weekend retreat. For more information on Alpha in North America, you can write them at 109 East 50th Street, New York, NY 10022, or contact them via telephone at (212) 378-0292.

In the early 1980's, the late John Wimber introduced mainstream evangelicalism to the terminology and method of "power evangelism."[10] In its broadest definition, this approach utilizes some kind of supernatural demonstration of the power of God such as signs and wonders, spiritual warfare, or gifts of the Spirit in order to create an opportunity in which to present the gospel. With its emphasis on miraculous prophetic insight, healing, or deliverance, power evangelism depends on supernatural phenomena in order to penetrate and break down resistance to the gospel message.

During times of divine visitation by the Holy Spirit there have also been displays of power as seen through deep conviction of sin, which left the person in a state of spiritual anguish and deep sorrow for his sins until he became converted. The conviction would be so strong that people would be reduced to tears, sometimes weeping and wailing over their eternal separation from God. During the First and Second Great Awakenings, the Cane Ridge Revival, and other revivals in Church history, power encounters were seen when the unregenerate were supernaturally knocked to the ground, causing them to jerk or tremble under deep conviction.

In recent years, many Christians have become interested in another facet of power evangelism called "strategic level spiritual warfare." Although there is a lot of diversity in its practice, the bottom line of this concept is the need to receive a victory in the heavenlies over a geographic area through dance, praise, declarative prayer, identificational repentance, and intercessory prayer. It presupposes that through various means God will lead the people of prayer to know what to strategically pray against. It is not only praying for God's blessing, but also for satan's binding. It does presuppose a power encounter in the heavenlies that affects the ability of unbelievers to accept or reject the claims of Christ.[11]

---

10.   John Wimber and Kevin Springer, *Power Evangelism* (San Francisco: Harper, 1992). Among the other very thoughtful works on the subject is *The Kingdom and the Power: Are Healing and Spiritual Gifts Used by Jesus and the Early Church Meant for the Church Today?*, edited by Gary S. Greig and Kevin N. Springer (Ventura, CA: Regal, 1993), and *Stories from the Front Lines: Power Evangelism in Today's World*, by Jane Rumph (Grand Rapids: Chosen, 1996).

11.   For more on this see "Spiritual Mapping Gains Credibility Among Leaders," by Art Moore in *Christianity Today*, January 12, 1998 (page 55), as well as the works of Dr. C. Peter Wagner, especially *Breaking Strongholds in Your City, Confronting the Powers* (Ventura, CA: Regal, 1993) and *Engaging the Enemy* (Ventura, CA: Regal, 1991). See also *The Twilight Labyrinth: Why Does Spiritual Darkness Linger Where It Does?* (Grand Rapids: Chosen, 1997) by George Otis Jr., and the book that lays down the biblical foundation for fighting the spiritual enemies of God: *God at War: The Bible and Spiritual Conflict* (Downers Grove, IL: InterVarsity, 1997) by Dr. Gregory Boyd. For the other side of this discussion see *Three Crucial Questions about Spiritual Warfare* (Grand Rapids: Baker, 1997) by Dr. Clinton E. Arnold.

One of the strategies of the enemy is to cause the Church to be divided over partial truths. It isn't that one of these methods and forms is right and the others are wrong. The truth is that all are valid forms of evangelism. Therefore, in discussing the blessing and potential blessing of power evangelism for reaching a post-modern world, do not hear a rejection of the other forms of evangelism. In fact, the harvest will be greatest when all are embraced and practiced by the Church.

Power Evangelism in the Early Church

The greatest example of power evangelism in the New Testament is the Ephesian revival (see Acts 19). Luke records the following about this move of God:

This went on for two years, so that all the Jews and Greeks who lived in the province of Asia heard the word of the Lord. God did extraordinary miracles through Paul, so that even handkerchiefs and aprons that had touched him were taken to the sick, and their illnesses were cured and the evil spirits left them (Acts 19:10-12).

So many people were becoming Christians that it was threatening the economic livelihood of the silversmiths who made their living from selling the idols of Artemis. Listen to the silversmith, Demetrius: "And you see and hear how this fellow Paul has convinced and led astray large numbers of people here in Ephesus and in practically the whole province of Asia..." (Acts 19:26). Church growth experts have said that this was Paul's greatest success, that the church at Ephesus could have been 50,000 strong by the time Timothy was overseeing it. Interestingly, this was also where Paul saw the greatest display of what we now call power evangelism. However, alongside the demonstrations of power, Paul was also involved in presentation evangelism.

Paul entered the synagogue and spoke boldly there for three months, arguing persuasively about the kingdom of God. But some of them became obstinate; they refused to believe and publicly maligned the Way. So Paul left them. He took the disciples with him and had discussions daily in the lecture hall of Tyrannus. This went on for two years, so that all the Jews and Greeks who lived in the province of Asia heard the word of the Lord (Acts 19:8-10).

Ephesus remains a stunning example of the use and success of power evangelism coupled with other methods in order to spread the gospel. It also prompts the question as to how the early Christians, who were without political power and considered practitioners of an illegal religion for part of the first several centuries, were successful in defeating the old religions and establishing Christianity as the religion of the Roman Empire. In his book *Christianizing the Roman Empire A.D. 100-400*,[12] Yale professor of history Ramsay MacMullen researched this question and discovered that the success of the early Church was not primarily due to great preaching or the result of the great apologists for the faith. Instead, it was primarily due to the results of power evangelism.

People became Christians because the Christian's God was more powerful than the false gods they were worshiping. This was evidenced in the power of God to heal and especially in the deliverance ministry of the Christians. Deliverance ministry was a reality in this time, even among other religions. What was so different, however, was how fast the Christians could bring deliverance to those who needed it. This discovery, that power evangelism was the context that allowed presentation evangelism to be more readily accepted by unbelievers, was not uncovered by a theologian or a Church historian, but rather a historian from Yale University.

Space does not permit a complete historical study of the role of power evangelism in the history of the Church's efforts to evangelize. Nevertheless, the historical record of Christianity clearly shows that aspects of power evangelism can be found right alongside other means of spreading the good news.

Within American Christian history, manifestations of the Holy Spirit's power within the context of evangelism can be seen in the writings of the First Great Awakening (1735-1742),[13] as well as in the record of the Second Great Awakening, especially in the Awakening's most famous meeting called the Cane Ridge Revival (1801).[14] These two awakenings both showcased power encounters such as falling, shaking, groaning, shouting, deliverance from demons, and falling into trances. These displays of the power of God were also evidenced within the lives of the

---

12.   Ramsay MacMullen, *Christianizing the Roman Empire (A.D. 100-400)* (New Haven, CT: Yale University Press, 1984), 62.

13.   For example, see Jonathan Edwards, *Jonathan Edwards on Revival* (Carlisle, PA: Banner of Truth, 1965).

14.   Paul K. Conkin, *Cane Ridge: America's Pentecost* (Madison, WI: University of Wisconsin Press, 1989).

early Methodist circuit riders,[15] as well as great revivalists such as Charles Gradison Finney.

The Pentecostal Revival, which many date back to January 1901, would again see manifestations of the Spirit's power such as people falling, shaking, rolling, weeping, wailing, dancing, laughing in the Spirit, and speaking in tongues. The Pentecostal Revival exploded in 1906 at a place called Azusa Street in Los Angeles. The first name for the Azusa Street Revival was the "Los Angeles Blessing."[16] Hungry people would travel from every inhabited continent to find more of the manifest presence of God and then return to spread the Pentecostal Revival in their country.

Rethinking Pentecostalism

Although I am not Pentecostal, I am grieved to realize how much prejudice there still is within the Body of Christ toward Pentecostalism. In my seminary course on evangelism, we studied every revival in North American Church history except two: the Pentecostal Revival and the Latter Rain Revival, which was Pentecostal in its origin. It is shameful that the most successful stream of the Church in reaching the lost during this century is rarely even mentioned in the evangelism courses of our evangelical seminaries and colleges. It is unhealthy to allow our prejudice to blind us to the fact of how powerfully God has used Pentecostals.

Despite the fact that Pentecostals in the early days were poor and had no institutions, buildings, money, or programs, they still reached more lost people than any other segment of the Church. Why? Because the Pentecostals embraced the outpouring of the Holy Spirit's power and the restoration of the ministries of the Holy Spirit (prophecy, tongues, interpretation, healing, and working of miracles) for our day. They understood that salvation includes not only the saving of the soul, but deliverance from demonized situations and healing of physical and emotional wounds. This is what gave such spiritual power to their message.

"Pentecostalism is the largest and most dynamic movement within evangelicalism," writes Australian researcher Mark Hutchinson in a recent issue of *Christianity Today*. "The explosive numerical growth and geographical expansion of Pentecostals in the last 30 years has given a new look to the religious make-up of the Third World—or the Two Thirds

---

15.   See, for example, John H. Wigger, *Taking Heaven by Storm: Methodism and the Rise of Popular Christianity in America* (New York: Oxford University Press, 1998).

16.   Vinson Synan shared this with me at a conference at my church in 1994.

World, as it is more accurately and positively called."[17] According to researcher David Barrett, two-thirds of Pentecostal and charismatic Christians can be found in Africa, Asia, and Latin America.[18] He also reports that this segment of Christianity is growing by 19 million per year.[19]

Ralph Martin has written one of the most powerful and honest books I have recently read, *The Catholic Church at the End of an Age: What Is the Spirit Saying?*[20] He notes that by 1982 the Pentecostal churches (not including the charismatics who have remained in traditional denominations) had become the largest body of Protestants— larger than the Baptists, Anglicans, Presbyterian, or Methodist churches. In Christendom, only the Roman Catholic Church has a larger following.[21] In 1992 the numbers of Pentecostals and charismatics had grown to more than 410 million and accounted for almost one-fourth of world Christianity.

"My research," writes Martin, "has led me to make this bold statement: In all of human history, no other non-political, non-militaristic, voluntary human movement has grown as rapidly as the Pentecostal-charismatic movement in the last 25 years."[22] As a Roman Catholic, he then makes the following observation: "...there is a message to which we need to pay attention. That message, in its simplest form, perhaps could be stated like this: *When Jesus is proclaimed clearly and confidently, in the power of the Holy Spirit, many more people come to faith and there is much more growth to the Church than when he is not.*"[23]

In the closing summary of his chapter on repentance, Martin asks:

"What might the Spirit be saying to the Catholic Church? A message as old and new as the day of Pentecost: Repent, believe, and you too will receive the gift of the Holy Spirit (Acts 2:38). Let us repent of any ways in which we have narrowed God, or limited him, in our thoughts, words, or actions. Let us repent of any ways we have obscured the central place

17.   Mark Hutchinson, "It's a Small Church After All," *Christianity Today*, November 16, 1998, 47.
18.   Hutchinson, "It's a Small Church," 47.
19.   David Barrett, "Pentecostals: World Growth at 19 Million a Year," *Christianity Today*, November 16, 1998, 28.
20.   Ralph Martin, *The Catholic Church at the End of an Age: What Is the Spirit Saying?* (San Francisco: Ignatius Press, 1994), 30.
21.   Martin, *The Catholic Church*, 86.
22.   Martin, *The Catholic Church*, 87.
23.   Martin, *The Catholic Church*, 118 (italics his).

of Jesus and put secondary things in his place. Let us repent of that 'ecclesio-centrism' that puts the Church in the place of Christ. Let us repent of any ways we have grieved the Holy Spirit and through our pride or fear resisted his workings."[24]

I have read few books where there is such a spirit of repentance. How I wish other churches had prophets who spoke so clearly to them. If the Roman Catholic Church has more people with a spirit similar to Ralph Martin's, then I believe it will see a great revival and will be used as a great harvester in the coming harvest.

"The church is a bride, and she shows to the world that her spouse is alive by living by his power and receiving life from him," Martin writes. "There is a danger in our day that the church will look more like a widow, alone and without resources except those possessed by any human organization. If we yield to what the Lord has poured out upon us—his Spirit—the world will know that the church is truly the spouse of a living Lord."[25]

The prophetic voice of Ralph Martin is speaking not just to the Roman Catholic Church, but to the entire Body of Christ. He is saying the harvest is upon us now. We do not have time to continue on as we have been. We must humble ourselves, repent of our wrongs as church bodies, and embrace the full ministry of the Holy Spirit with all His gifts.

Harvey Cox approaches his assessment of Pentecostalism from a completely different angle than does Ralph Martin. He is a professor of religion at Harvard University and the author of more than ten books, including the best-selling 1960's classic, *The Secular City*. Ironically, the predictions made in *The Secular City* failed to come about. The culture of the world has not become more secular; rather, it has become more spiritual, though not always more Christian. Post-modern thought has rejected the closed worldview of the secular city and has embraced a world closer to the worldview of the first century than probably any other century in the last 500 years.

Nowhere is this more evidenced than in Cox's new book, *Fire From Heaven: The Rise of Pentecostal Spirituality and the Reshaping of Religion in the Twenty-first Century*. Interestingly enough, it is Cox's admission of having been wrong. But, it is more than that. Where *The Secular City* thought

---

24.   Martin, *The Catholic Church*, 164.
25.   Martin, *The Catholic Church*, 198-99.

that Christianity would not be able to hold the city, causing the growing metropolises to become increasingly more secular, *Fire From Heaven* is the study of why Pentecostal and charismatic churches have thrived in the context of the city. When *The Secular City* was written, Cox was noting the demise of the institutional church in the changing neighborhoods of the city. He was noting the death of large older mainline churches; therefore, he concluded the church would lose the cities of the world. Cox's problem was not seeing how God would raise up the Pentecostal and charismatic churches and then, through their weakness, reveal His strength.

Looking deeply and honestly at the evidence, Cox now eloquently states the case like this:

"The signs and wonders that appeared at Azusa Street and in the global movement it loosed included far more than speaking in tongues. People danced, leaped, and laughed in the Spirit, received healings, fell into trances, and felt themselves caught up into a transcendent sphere. In retrospect we can also describe the revival as the principal point in western history at which the pulsating energy of African American spirituality, wedded by years of suffering to the Christian promise of the Kingdom of God, leaped across the racial barrier and became fused with similar motifs in the spirituality of poor white people. It marked the breaking of the barrier that western civilization had so carefully erected between the cognitive and the emotional sides of life, between rationality and symbol, between the conscious and unconscious strata of the mind. In this context, the mixing of the races was not just an early equal opportunity program. It had powerful archetypal significance as well. It presaged a new world in which both the outer and the inner divisions of humankind would be abolished, and it was the harbinger of one of the great surprises of the twentieth century, the massive and unanticipated resurgence of religion in a century many had thought would witness its withering away."[26]

---

26.   Harvey Cox, *Fire From Heaven: The Rise of Pentecostal Spirituality and the Reshaping of Religion in the Twenty-First Century* (New York: Addison-Wesley Publishing Co., 1994), 99-100.

Signs, Wonders, and Church Growth Around the World

On the continent of Africa there are over 5,000 independent, Pentecostal-oriented Christian denominations, all born within the last 100 years. These sub-Saharan Christian churches are growing faster than Islam, almost twice as fast as the Roman Catholic Church, and almost three times as fast as the non-Catholic, non-Pentecostal churches. For example, these churches account for 40 percent of the black population in South Africa and 50 percent of the Christians in Zimbabwe. "At present rates of growth," writes Harvey Cox, "by the year 2,000 these churches will include more members in Africa than either the Roman Catholic Church or all the Protestant denominations put together."[27]

Why these churches have been so successful is a complex question. Nevertheless, if you ask what one factor drew the people to first attend one of these churches, the answer is healing. According to Cox's assessment of the research, "These indigenous Christian churches provide a setting in which the African conviction that spirituality and healing belong together is dramatically enacted. The typical disciple comes to such a church for the first time in search of healing, usually for a malady that has resisted either traditional or modern medicine or both."[28]

"Our efforts to come to grasp with the necessity of addressing felt needs of the people eventually launched us into power evangelism," says William F. Kumuyi, pastor of Deeper Life Bible Church with an adult membership of more than 85,000 at its international headquarters in Gbagada, Lagos, Nigeria.[29]

Combined with a strong emphasis on holiness of life and conduct, the Deeper Life Bible Church uses miracles to attract unbelievers. Thursday evenings are their night for praying for the miraculous, with several thousand in attendance. "The ministry time became the high point, and the miracles that followed were used by God to attract more who were in need," reports Kumuyi. "This became a regular feature of ministry in Deeper Life, creating a public reputation and awakening interest in the deeper things of God among the members. Ministries of the miraculous are particularly relevant to African situations, especially needs for deliverance, healing, and material provision."[30]

---

27.   Cox, *Fire From Heaven*, 246.
28.   Cox, *Fire From Heaven*, 247.
29.   William F. Kumuyi, "Deeper Christian Life Ministry," *The New Apostolic Churches*, edited by C. Peter Wagner (Ventura, CA: Regal, 1998), 248.
30.   Kumuyi, "Deeper Christian Life Ministry," *The New Apostolic Churches*, 253-54.

Dr. C. Peter Wagner reports on one of the events that they have seen in Nigeria.

"Part of the usual weekly program in all of the 4,500 Deeper Life Bible Churches is a Thursday-night miracle meeting. On one of those nights, the pastor of an outlying church felt led to invite all those who had sick people at home to hold up their handkerchiefs, and he prayed a blessing of God's healing power upon them. They were to return home, place the handkerchief on the sick person and pray for healing in Jesus' name. He was unaware that the chief of a nearby Muslim village was visiting his church that night—the first time he had ever attended a Christian service. Although the Muslim did not have sick people in his home, he also held up his handkerchief and received the blessing. Soon after the chief had returned to his village, a nine-year-old girl died and he went to her home to attend the wake just before the burial. While there, he suddenly remembered the handkerchief, retrieved it, placed it on the corpse and prayed that she would be healed in Jesus' name. Then God did an obviously 'unusual' miracle and raised the girl from the dead! The chief called an immediate ad hoc meeting with the village elders who had witnessed what had happened, then turned around and declared to his people: 'For many years we have been serving Mohammed; but from this moment on our village will be a village of Jesus!' Needless to say, a Deeper Life Bible Church is now thriving in the village."[31]

Several years ago I invited Pastor Dion Robert from Abidjan, Ivory Coast, to preach in my church in St. Louis, Missouri. At that time in the early 1990's, his church numbered over 20,000 and was growing rapidly. His ministry is noted for its signs and wonders, healings, miracles, and deliverance. It is one of the largest churches in the Franco-speaking world. It is also a cell church that teaches people to expect miracles in their cell groups. Pastor Robert tells the story of one teen cell group that prayed for a dead person who was brought back to life. Today, the church has over 100,000 people in attendance.

---

31.   C. Peter Wagner, *Blazing the Way, Book 3, Acts 15–28* (Ventura, CA: Regal, 1995), 166.

The dramatic growth among churches that embrace the powerful ministry of the Holy Spirit extends far beyond the African continent. In nations such as England, Canada, and Australia, Spirit-filled churches have been growing and thriving while those representing mainline Protestantism and Catholicism have shown steady decline.[32] Churches such as Matthew Ashimolowo's Kingsway International Christian Centre,[33] Sandy Millar's Holy Trinity Brompton Anglican Church in London,[34] John Arnott's Toronto Airport Christian Fellowship, and Frank Houston's New Life Church in Sydney continue to grow as they pursue the supernatural ministry of healing and deliverance.

Throughout Asia, the largest and most influential churches in most of the nations are Pentecostal or charismatic. The Yoido Full Gospel Church pastored by David Yonggi Cho in Seoul, Korea, has more than 800,000 members and is widely regarded as the largest church in the world. In Singapore, Lawrence Khong pastors Faith Community Baptist Church, an enormous cell-group congregation that pursues the ministry of the Holy Spirit. The Church of Our Savior, an Anglican church, is also found in Singapore. Several thousand members attend this charismatic church pastored by the Rev. Derek Hong.

---

32. According to Harvey Cox, survey data on many churches in England between 1985 and 1990 indicates that the Baptists, Methodists, Presbyterians, Anglicans, and Roman Catholics all lost members. The Catholic and the Anglican numbers were down about 10 percent within the five-year period. However, the independent churches during the same time frame, comprised mostly of Pentecostal and charismatic churches, had grown by 30 percent. (*Fire from Heaven*, 187.)

    Ralph Martin includes some statistics for Australian growth rates from 1976 through 1981: the United Church, -10 percent; Anglican, 5 percent; Churches of Christ, 8 percent; Lutheran, 10 percent; Roman Catholic, 24 percent; Baptist, 24 percent; Pentecostal, 385 percent. In nearby New Zealand, for the period 1971–1981, it was worse: Methodist, -19 percent; Presbyterian, -11 percent; Anglican, -9 percent; Roman Catholic, 2 percent; Baptist, 6 percent; Associated Pentecostal, 150 percent. (*The Catholic Church at the End of an Age*, 88-89.)

33. The *London Times* reported in August 1998 on the Kingsway International Christian Centre and Pastor Matthew Ashimolowo, a former Muslim. The paper stated that the 5,500-member Pentecostal church is thought to be "the largest independent church to open in Britain for more than a century." (Clive Price, "London's Fastest Growing Church Has International Flavor," *Charisma*, March 1999, 36-37.)

34. At one point in 1994 the lines outside Holy Trinity Brompton were so long to get into the church because of Toronto Blessing-oriented renewal services, that tickets were given out to allow people to get into the church.

Campus Crusade's Bill Bright[35] and Dr. C. Peter Wagner[36] have both reported on the occurrence of visions and dreams being used by the Holy Spirit to lead Muslims throughout the Middle East to Jesus Christ. Others have noticed it as well. "Every Arabic Christian I have talked to who converted to Christ from a non-Christian background relates a dream or vision in which Jesus, dressed in white as in the Transfiguration, speaks directly to them, telling them he is the Savior of the world," reports evangelist Luis Palau in *Christianity Today.* "A woman whose father is a top leader in her nation—a nation where there are no church

---

35.   In a letter from Bill Bright regarding the JESUS film dated August 1995, he reports that the Middle East Campus Crusade office is receiving thousands of letters from Muslims, many of them telling about a dream they had: "I saw Jesus. He declared to me 'I am the way.' "

   "In Algeria, a number of people discovered they had the very same dream," writes Bright. "They began to talk with one another and discovered each had experienced the same dream. The details were the same, and even the words Jesus said to them were the same. On their own, they have formed a Bible study and are following Christ!" He also tells the story of a Muslim woman who spent four years in prison for her political activities. "While there, Jesus appeared to her in her cell," says Bright. "He personally explained redemption and the Gospel." She is now on the Campus Crusade staff.

36.   On page 3 of the October 1995 *Prayer Track News,* the newsletter of the AD 2000 & Beyond Movement, Dr. C. Peter Wagner of Fuller Theological Seminary reports on an incredible story of a rich man in a Muslim country who brought his very sick daughter to a Christian hospital. "The daughter had been paralyzed for four years. They put her in a private room which had a cross hanging on the wall. The man, a very devout Muslim, demanded that the cross be taken down at once. Reverently, they took the cross off the wall because the Christian staff working there was threatened for witnessing in a Muslim country. That evening, the Christian nurse, in her own quiet way, told the sick girl that Christ died on the cross for our sins and he can forgive her sins and heal her.

   "The girl could not sleep that night because she had so many questions. *'He can heal me? Who is he and where is he? What is this mystery of the cross? Why was my father so angry and so afraid of this cross?'* With tears streaming down her cheeks she longed to know more about Isa (Jesus). In the quiet of that night, she saw a figure clothed in white. He had a halo of light around his head that filled the whole room. Then she heard His voice, 'Get up and put the cross back on the wall.' With fear and trembling she said, 'I cannot walk.' Jesus then revealed himself to her and told her, 'I am Jesus who died on the cross, but I am alive. Get up and walk.' She got up and took the cross from under her bed and put it back on the wall. Then she turned, but the Lord was no longer there. Realizing what had just happened, she started shouting, 'I saw Isa and he healed me! I can walk, I can walk!' She called her father who rushed to the hospital and witnessed what had happened. With tears in his eyes, all he could say was, 'I want to know more about Jesus.' "

buildings—was converted through a dream in which Jesus revealed himself. The first five years of her Christian life she didn't even have a Bible."

Palau continues: "Christians in the Middle East, many of whom are respected professionals with postgraduate degrees, expect God to work this way. They believe in his supernatural intervention. If God is God, he is going to do supernatural things. No barriers can thwart or frustrate God's redemptive plan."[37]

From personal experience, I have seen the effect of power evangelism in South America. In 1997 I spent two weeks in Chile, Argentina, and Uruguay. During that 14-day period we saw almost 2,000 people healed, hundreds saved, and scores delivered. For me, this was an eye-opening experience.

While in Chile, I visited the Templo Centro Metropolitano in Santiago. This church is pastored by Fernando Chaparros, a former police officer. Although it was only a few years old, it had more than 10,000 in attendance and was the second largest church in the nation. Needless to say, it is a church that emphasizes the power of the Holy Spirit through healing and deliverance.

Our host in Uruguay was Pastor Jorge Marquez. In a country that had not had a Protestant church grow past 500, Marquez leads a congregation in Montevideo of 3,000. Since the church was so large and was only a few years old, I asked him how he planted it and why it was so successful in reaching the masses. Pastor Marquez told me the church had been built on advertisements promising healing and deliverance from demonic strongholds. There are now six young pastors helping him with the 28 preaching services per week. Every one of these pastors had been addicted to drugs and/or alcohol and needed deliverance when he first met them.

Like so many other North Americans attest, my time in Argentina would prove to be most fruitful.[38] While I was there, I had the pleasure of meeting one of the elder statesmen of the Argentine revival, Dr. Omar Cabrera, Sr., the leader of a network of churches throughout Argentina called Vision of the Future. His home church numbers over

---

37. *Christianity Today*, November 16, 1998, 76.
38. I highly recommend *The Rising Revival: Firsthand Accounts of the Incredible Argentine Revival—And How It Can Spread throughout the World*, edited by C. Peter Wagner and Pablo Deiros (Ventura, CA: Regal, 1998). This book contains chapters from Carlos Annacondia, Pablo Bottari, Omar Cabrera, Claudio Freidzon, Carlos Mraida, Eduardo Lorenzo, and many other contributors.

80,000 and meets in over 200 congregations in many cities in Argentina. His churches were the easiest congregations I have ever ministered in for healing. The churches were founded on Omar's healing and miracle anointing, and the people understood the word of knowledge's relationship to healing and were full of faith.

In the city of Cordoba, I was asked to preach in a Vision of the Future church that met in an old, barn-like building. We saw 800 people give testimony to being healed in one meeting, including a woman who had been blind for three years due to a retina being destroyed from diabetes. The night before, another woman was healed of deafness and blindness on one side of her head. The pastor told me that if we could stay, the crowds would grow to over 10,000. In order to honor other commitments, I made the mistake of leaving. Looking back on it, I wish I would have stayed.

While in Argentina I met the co-pastors of the Central Baptist Church of Buenos Aries, Drs. Pablo Deiros and Carlos Mraida (both of whom have made contributions to this book). Their church had seen more church plants and people go into ministry during the last four years than it had seen in the previous 100 years. Why? Because the church had been open and hungry for the recent visitation of the Spirit in their church, characterized by healing, manifestations of the Holy Spirit, and deliverance. Their church was the second church in the city to receive the fresh anointing of the Holy Spirit. It is the oldest Baptist church in Argentina and the second largest in that country.

Dr. Deiros told me that about 70 percent of the Baptist churches in Argentina were now embracing the ministry of healing and deliverance. Victor Lorenzo, son of Eduardo Lorenzo, an influential Baptist leader in Argentina, told me that the Baptists had to move from their former opposition to the gifts of the Spirit or they were going to lose their people to the Pentecostals.

The Iglesia "Rey de Reyes" (King of Kings Church) has grown from 6 to over 8,000 since God freshly anointed Pastor Claudio Freidzon for healing and power evangelism. I have both visited and preached in his Assembly of God church. It has an atmosphere of expectation for the presence of God to visit the congregation and touch the people with healing, deliverance, and a refreshing anointing of joy and peace.[39]

---

39.   See Claudio Freidzon's book, *Holy Spirit, I Hunger For You* (Orlando, FL: Creation House, 1997).

While I was in Buenos Aires, I also visited and spoke in Guillermo Prein's New Life Church. It regularly has over 3,000 in attendance. It was founded by having healing and deliverance meetings in a very dangerous park in the city. They now have meetings 21 times per week, even a service at 3:00 a.m. for the taxicab drivers. This church has the reputation for having the most healings occur during their services. Interestingly, over 60 percent of them occur when the children 12 and younger pray. While I was there I asked one of the associate pastors, "So, what do you do?" He said, "My job is to verify the miracles." I asked, "What else?" He responded, "My job is to verify the miracles." They have verification of a woman who had a hysterectomy, was prayed for by the children, and now has given birth to a child. She received a creative miracle.

In Guatemala, Harold Cabelleros pastors a church that now has an attendance over 8,000. El Shaddai Church is one of the fastest growing churches in the country. The congregation believes in and practices healing, deliverance, and other demonstrations of God's power, both in the services and in the cell groups. Pastor Harold also believes that the growth of the church is related to the strategic-level spiritual warfare that is practiced by selected individuals of the church.

On a recent ministry trip to Brazil, I saw once again the tremendous power of the Holy Spirit to transform lives. I was invited to preach by the leaders of the Foursquare Church of Sao Paulo and Belo Horizonte. The pastors and leaders in Brazil are among the hungriest I have ever met for more of God. The outpouring of the Spirit was extremely powerful, and the healing anointing was the second strongest I have experienced in my life. Only in Cordoba, Argentina, a few years previous, did I see a stronger anointing for healing.

Elsewhere in Brazil, the Assemblies of God denomination is growing rapidly and numbers between 11 to 15 million members. This is the fruit from the ministry of two men who brought the Pentecostal message to Brazil at the early part of this century. Today scholars believe there are more Pentecostals at church on Sunday than there are Roman Catholics attending mass.

A similar picture is emerging all over Latin America. In his book *Is Latin America Turning Protestant?* David Stoll pulls together statistics from a number of sources to show that non-Catholic Christianity is growing in many of the continent's countries at five or six times the rate of the general population. If the statistics in Brazil are any indication, 90 percent of this non-Catholic increase is Pentecostal. Stoll predicts that if current rates of growth continue, five or six Latin American countries will have non-Catholic—mostly Pentecostal—majorities by 2010. In several other nations the non-Catholic percentage of the population will have reached 30-40 percent.[40]

In my opinion, Colombia is the ripest nation for revival in the Western hemisphere. While in Argentina meeting with leaders of the revival, I was told by one of them that the real revival is in Colombia, "where they are still killing the pastors." Shortly thereafter I was invited to preach in Bogota, Medillin, and Cali. Prior to going to Columbia, one of my friends who had preached there warned me that I would think they didn't understand the gospel invitation because so many would accept the invitation. He was right. We saw 454 people commit to Christ for the first time in their lives, 1,750 rededicated from backslidden conditions, and almost 1,200 healed; and over 350 responded to ministry for deliverance. The deliverance ministry occurred in only two of the 16 meetings in 10 days. I did think that they misunderstood the invitation, but they hadn't. They were merely hungry for God.

In January 1999 my team met with Cesar Castellanos, pastor of The International Charismatic Mission in Bogota, Columbia. He was born into the Kingdom of God through hearing the audible voice of God and then experiencing His presence come into his room. His church experiences healings, and they have an "encounter weekend" for new believers where they are taken through inner healing and deliverance and receive the baptism in the Holy Spirit and the vision for the church. He now has a church of 27,000 cell groups. They don't know exactly how many people are in the church at this time because they count the number of groups, not the individuals. However, the groups usually average about 10. Not long ago, he and his wife were shot in an assassination attempt. While they were recuperating for 11 months, the church grew by 100,000 while being led by the youth pastor. This is the fastest growing church in the Western hemisphere. They believe in spiritual warfare through prayer, dancing, praise, fasting, and intercessory prayer. They meet three times per Sunday in the coliseum of Bogota.

North America, along with Western Europe, has long been considered by some to be the Nazareth of the Church world. We are a nation of skeptics, and proud of it. Regardless of the evangelists whom I have spoken with, I hear the same report—they do not see the same degree of healing and miracles here that they do in non-western countries. I long for the day when that is no longer true.

---

40.   Cox, *Fire From Heaven*, 168.

In a study of recognized Christian denominations in the U.S. and Canada between 1965 and 1989, the following rates of decline and growth were reported. Those declining included the Disciples of Christ, -45 percent; Presbyterian, -32 percent; Episcopal, -29 percent, United Church, -21 percent; United Methodist, -19 percent; Evangelical Lutheran, -8 percent. Those growing included the Roman Catholic Church, 23 percent; Southern Baptist, 38 percent; Church of the Nazarene, 63 percent; Seventh Day Adventist, 92 percent; Assemblies of God (Pentecostal), 121 percent; Church of God (Pentecostal), 183 percent.[41]

The fastest growth among the North American churches has been the thousands of new charismatic churches. Apostolic networks numbering thousands of churches have developed during the past 20 years. Most of these networks of churches would embrace the dynamic of power evangelism with its primary focus on healing and deliverance.[42]

Based upon numerous studies, the Church is growing the fastest in most places of the world where there is an openness to and the practice of power evangelism. I believe that as the world becomes more postmodern in its worldview, those churches that are open to power encounters will be best suited to have an impact upon their communities. The old apologetic, which was based entirely upon presentation evangelism, needs to be augmented by utilizing displays of power with the explanation of the gospel. Although presence evangelism softens the hearts of the unbelievers, making it easier for them to be open to the gospel, in order to be most effective in reaching the masses—especially those in the 10/40 window—we also need to embrace ministry such as healing and deliverance and not be afraid of the phenomena that can accommodate the visitation of God's empowering presence.

I believe that God is preparing the Church through the Holy Spirit in these last days for one of the most powerful revivals in human history. Perhaps this revival is already happening in parts of the earth. More people are alive right now who have not heard the gospel than have lived and died in the history of humanity. Just before he died, the great

---

41.   Martin, *The Catholic Church*, 90. Though I have been emphasizing the growth of movements as a sign of the ability of the movement to draw people, I realize it does not vindicate the group as an orthodox Christian group. Heresies can grow fast also. To illustrate this point, this data also reports that the second fastest-growing group was the Mormon cult at 133 percent.

42.   For more information on these networks, see *The New Apostolic Churches*, edited by C. Peter Wagner (Ventura: CA: Regal, 1998).

Pentecostal evangelist Smith Wigglesworth told Lester Sumrall about a coming revival. Sumrall related this experience in these words:

"I see it!"

"What do you see?"

"I see a revival coming to planet Earth, as never before. There will be untold multitudes who will be saved. No man will say, 'So many and so many,' because no man will be able to count those who will come to Jesus Christ. *I see it!* The dead will be raised, the arthritic healed, cancer will be healed. No disease will be able to stand before God's people, and it will spread all over the world. It will be a worldwide thrust of God's power and a thrust of God's anointing. I will not see it, but you will see it."[43]

What if Wigglesworth was right? I pray he was. And I want to see it.

---

43.   Ron McIntosh, *The Quest For Revival: Experiencing Great Revivals of the Past, Empowering You for God's Move Today!* (Tulsa, OK: Harrison House, 1994), 13-14.

"My heart's desire is to answer the cry of the poor for God and the cry of God for the poor," says Chris Heuertz. *He is the executive director of Word Made Flesh, an organization focused on serving Jesus among the poorest of the poor. The ministry provides relief, development help, and care for women and children in developing countries. Word Made Flesh also organizes servant teams that go out in six-month commitments to minister.*

Not only does Chris care for the poor, but he also cares for the Church who has forgotten the poor. He feels it is time to wake up a slumbering Church to the needs outside of her gates. In 1997 Chris was ordained as a minister through the Association of Evangelical Churches and Ministries, and he and his wife Phileena travel extensively, sharing what God is doing through and among the poor peoples of the earth.

Chapter 6

Discovering Holiness in Ministry Among the Poor

by Chris Heuertz

My apartment in India was located at the end of a dirt road in a community known as "Majestic Colony." Every time I needed to go somewhere or get something, I had to walk 150 yards down this road and turn left toward the markets and stores.

Halfway along the journey the road became paved, but the area was still extremely poor. On both sides of the street were houses, shacks, slums, and structures inhabited by families struggling to stay alive. There were piles of trash and waste swept to the side of the street. The area looked devastated, the way you'd imagine a street would look like after a war.

It was a pretty cheerless and dismal street, a stark example of the urban residential poverty of India. If it weren't for the little children playing blissfully along the road, it would have been a very depressing area.

There was one small child who became my special friend. I would usually make a point to look for her if she didn't find me first. Her name was Prabah. She was eight years old and as cute as a button. She had big, gorgeous brown eyes, long eyelashes, long stringy black hair, high cheekbones, and she was missing her left front tooth.

Prabah's family was wonderful. She was the youngest of five daughters: Sujata was 20, Indu Madi was 18, Radicah was 16, Ramya was 11, and Prabah was 8. Both of their parents worked very hard. Their father was a construction worker, and their mother made and sold long strings of tiny jasmine flowers that women wore in their hair.

Their home was a little thatch-roofed shanty constructed in the seven feet between two old, dilapidated brick houses. That was where they ate, slept, cooked their food, did their homework, played their games, and prayed before their idol of Ganesh (the elephant-headed god of "prosperity").

They became a sort of family to me. Occasionally, I'd stop by in the evenings to share a cup of tea with their father, trying to battle through his limited English and my even more limited Tamil. I would play jacks with the girls or look at the 15 family photos that they cherished as their most prized possessions. Their little home in the slums had been a refuge for me in many times of frustration.

There was one night that I'll never forget. It was dark. They did not have electricity in their home even when the power was on, so they depended on the streetlights for some of their light. They had two small candles burning, casting a dim, golden light on the dirty walls and dirt floor. They sat me down on the only stool in the place, and we tried to talk. A little Tamil here and a little English there, and we knew, more or less, that everyone was okay and doing well. Then the girls invited me to stay for dinner.

So many times I had walked by and they had asked, "*Saap teeng lah?*" (Have you eaten?), and just as many times as they had asked, they had invited me to join them for lunch or dinner. Every time I declined. It wasn't that I didn't want to eat with them. It was that I always felt they needed all the food they had, and sharing with me would only mean that they'd go without. This time, however, I felt that I needed to stay.

I tried to help Indu Madi and Radicah cook. There wasn't much that I could help with. They had a few worn-out, metal vessels to cook dinner in and an open fire in the corner. First, they cooked a big pot of plain rice, and then they started on the curry. Since I was there, they wanted to give me the best, so Ramya ran to the store to get a few eggs.

There wasn't a lot of food, but it took an hour to prepare the meal. When it was ready, we sat cross-legged on the dirt floor and Indu Madi served us. We each received a few spoons of plain rice and then a very small portion of egg curry to mix in with the rice. My heart broke as she served us. The girls hardly had anything for themselves, yet they were so happy to share with me. We sat together, barefoot, eating with our hands, happy and content. There wasn't much flavor to the rice—the curry just helped it go down easier—but it was a priceless communion that satisfied my soul.

When everyone had eaten, we sat around and listened to some soft Tamil music on an old, beat-up transistor radio. It was perfect. The later it got, the more sleepy we all became, and soon it was time to lay the little girls down to sleep. I said good night and walked past the gate into "Majestic Colony," back to my home.

I laid down on my bed and with a candle burning beside me said a prayer for my little friends—my friends who work harder, but eat less than anyone I know; my friends who give so much, but get so very little; my friends who seem to have so much joy, despite their poverty; my friends who were sleeping on the ground and who were probably still hungry.

I open with this story to illustrate a point. The Church, for the most part, living in "Majestic Colony," has mistaken God's financial blessings as individual provision rather than resources with potential for Kingdom development. With this misunderstanding has come an unwillingness to recognize and identify with Jesus' model of ministry and application of holiness.

In a proper understanding of the nature of holiness, it is imperative that the Church embrace a heart of compassion and respond to the call of Kingdom justice.

As holiness is cultivated in our lives, our relationships and perceptions of the poor will be the perfect testing ground validating God's redemptive work of sanctification.

During many of my conversations with Mother Teresa, she repeatedly shared that we need the poor so much more than they need us. She is right. God often uses the poor to induce social holiness. From the example of the poor we are humbled. Through the example of the weak, the foolish, the lowly, and the despised, we are instructed. The poor have a lot to teach us, yet our pride often prevents us from learning from them.

The faith of the North American Church has become very exclusive. If someone does not fit the social and economic mold of our churches, they may have a tough time being accepted by Christians. As a Church, we must learn new ways to celebrate our faith inclusively so that those on the margins of society will feel welcome in our churches and in our communities, and so that our love and acceptance of the other will produce holiness.

How many of us belong to a congregation that wouldn't stare at a prostitute if he or she walked into the sanctuary on Sunday morning? One that would not wonder why he or she was there? One that would not judge or criticize him or her in our hearts and minds? The prostitutes of first-century Palestine felt as if they could spend time with Jesus—why can't they feel the same way with His followers?

The Biblical Witness

Jesus' ministry was not to the upper class, the educated, the elite, or the most influential social figures. Jesus came and ministered among the poor, with the poor, and as a poor man. His ministry was to the children, the beggars, the lepers, the despised woman at the well, the adulteress caught in her sin, the tax collectors, the fishermen communities, the sinners, and the marginalized. Jesus came to the common people and lived alongside them.

Jesus' ministry was marked with a distinctive compassion for the poor. The first recorded words coming from the mouth of Jesus as He began His public ministry are found in Luke 4:18-19. Jesus entered the synagogue, unrolled the scrolls of Isaiah, and read the fulfilled prophecy:

> *The Spirit of the Lord is on Me, because He has anointed Me to preach good news to the poor. He has sent Me to proclaim freedom for the prisoners and recovery of sight for the blind, to release the oppressed, to proclaim the year of the Lord's favor.*

In the Gospel of Matthew, we find Jesus identifying Himself with the afflictions and sufferings of the poor. In Matthew 25:42-43 we read the familiar passage,

> *For I was hungry and you gave Me nothing to eat, I was thirsty and you gave Me nothing to drink, I was a stranger and you did not invite Me in, I needed clothes and you did not clothe Me, I was sick and in prison and you did not look after Me.*

As we look upon the faces of the poor; as we see the children, the beggars on the streets, and those in need; we are being confronted by Christ. He is placing before us an opportunity to serve Him and to love Him. He is giving us an opportunity to love Him and give back to Him through the vessel of the impoverished.

He was approached by the religious, the educated, and even the rich. Who can forget His encounter with the rich young ruler: "Go sell everything you have and give it to the poor...then come and follow Me" (see Mt. 19:21; Mk. 10:21).[1] When John's disciples were sent to question if Jesus was the Christ, the response sent in return was "...the good news is preached to the poor" (Mt. 11:5). In Luke, Jesus states in the beatitudes, "...Blessed are you who are poor, for yours is the kingdom of God" (Lk. 6:20).

The gospel clearly shows us the love and compassion that God has for the poor. From the beginning to the end, the Bible is full of references to the poor.

In the Old Testament, the laws of Deuteronomy show a special concern for the poor.[2] The poetic literature of the Psalms portrays God as a defender of the defenseless and a father to the fatherless.[3] The wisdom of Proverbs defines a generous man as one who shares with the poor. Passages in Proverbs illustrate God's love for the poor.[4] The prophets close the Old Testament with strong words of judgment on a nation that had turned its back on God and closed its ears to the cries of the poor.[5]

If we look through the rest of the New Testament, we continue to find references to our brothers and sisters in need. In the Book of James we find a letter full of references to the poor and how we should conduct ourselves on their behalf. James reminds us of the life that we are called to live:

> *Religion that God our Father accepts as pure and faultless is this: to look after orphans and widows in their distress and to keep oneself from being polluted by the world* (James 1:27).

What Is Poverty?

The Scriptures have plenty to say about the poor, but what is poverty? What are the issues involved? The definition of poverty would have to include, but should not be limited to, concepts such as marginalization,

---

1.   For compelling commentary on this passage, see Chapter 3 in *Wealth as Peril and Obligation: The New Testament on Possessions* by Sondra Ely Wheeler (Grand Rapids: Eerdmans Publishing Company, 1995), 39-56.

2.   See Deut. 14:28-29; 15:7-11; 16:11-14,18; 24:14-15,17-21.

3.   See Ps. 10:14; 41:1; 68:5-6; 109:6-16; 132:15; 146:7.

4.   See Prov. 14:31; 19:17; 21:13; 22:9; 28:5; 29:7; 31:8-9.

5.   See Is. 1:17; 3:14-15; 11:1-5; 28:17; 58:5-10; Jer. 2:34; 5:27-28; 7:5-7; 22:3,16; 49:11; Ezek. 16:49; Hos. 2:19; 10:12; Amos 5:7,10-15,24; 8:4-6; Mic. 2:1-3; 3:1-3; Hab. 1:3-4; Zech. 7:10.

lack of opportunity, lack of sustainable access to resources, and an inability to change circumstances. If these aspects are accepted as elements in a multi-variable causation of poverty, then every society and every culture contains the poor. And if these aspects are accepted as elements in a multi-variable causation of poverty, then, unfortunately, the Church has too often contributed to the crisis.

There are six issues that have hindered the Church from effectively ministering among and with the poor.

1. Isolation

On one level the Church has isolated herself from the poor. It can be said that we worship in a soundproof glass sanctuary. As the statistics of poverty grow, the Church only sings louder so as not to hear the staggering numbers or their cries.

I believe that God is using the cries of the poor today to call His Church out of her soundproof sanctuaries. He is challenging the Church to respond to a world in need. Too often, however, the Church has isolated herself and failed to listen, and thus contributed to the suffering.

In the isolation of the poor and the insulation from the poor, the individual members of the Church have caused a deep fragmentation and division within the corporate members of the Church. This fractured fragmentation and division of community poses a problem in light of an impoverished world. Because of isolation and insulation, the lack of community offered to the poor is yet another cause of marginalization and, in turn, a cause of poverty.

On another level, the Church often isolates the poor. I have walked out of countless churches in India, only to be greeted by a long line of beggars waiting at the gate of the building. These men and women know "their place"—they stand outside the gates. Do our multi-million dollar sanctuaries in North America send the same message?

There is also a popular misunderstanding that financial blessing is an indication of right standing before God. This leads to the judgment that the poor are outside right relationship with God. The assumption is made that when the poor are saved, their financial problems will be cured. Obviously this is not true, but those who hold to this belief isolate the poor by placing unfounded judgment on their spirituality because of their physical conditions. This misconception—that poverty is a judgment of God as a result of broken relationship with God—strips compassion and denies the poor God's love and mercy.

2. Fractured Community

I've visited many fishing villages in South India to find one consistent reality. Among a predominantly Hindu village there will be perhaps 100 Muslims and one mosque, and there will be 40 Christians and five churches. These churches will be from among the various denominations of the region and will have very little tolerance for one another.

While Christianity is fractured, the Muslims, who are famous for brotherhood, take the appealing edge. The poor need community. They have nothing but each other. They find strength in numbers. How can the Church expect the poor to join her, if she can't offer them the one thing they know they need?

These first issues, *isolation* and *fractured community*, both communicate themselves in terms of a broken relationship between the poor and the Church. Until this relationship is healed and we initiate reconciliation between God and man, there can be no progress.

3. Selfishness

In too many instances, the Church has been tight-fisted and stingy. It is so tempting to simply make more and give less. Mother Teresa said, "If the poor die of hunger, it is not because God does not care for them. Rather, it is because neither you nor I are generous enough."[6]

In a world where the chasm between the rich and the poor grows wider, it is imperative that the Church reach out in willingness to share the financial blessings God has graciously poured upon her. According to current United Nations Development Program figures, "The richest 20 percent of the world's population receives 82.7 percent of the total world income while the poorest 20 percent receives only 1.4 percent. Global economic growth rarely filters down."[7]

In the context of a dying world, the Church must redefine her spirituality and her understanding of holiness as it relates to justice. Part of that redefining process must involve a reversal in our understanding of finances. If the Church continues to hold tightly to her material wealth, the poor will continue to go without. Selfishness only contributes to the global disparity that excludes the poor and, in part, defines as well as perpetuates poverty.

6.　Mother Teresa, *No Greater Love*, eds. Beck Benenate and Joseph Durepos (Novato, CA: New World Library, 1992), 40-41.

7.　Frances O'Gorman, *Charity and Change: From Bandaid to Beacon* (Victoria, Australia: World Vision Australia, 1992), 67.

4. Paternalism

One prevalent belief that hinders effective ministry is the assumed position that the poor cannot help themselves. Oftentimes churches develop projects and programs that impose themselves upon the poor. In defining poverty, a portion of that definition should include the aspect that explains poverty as "the inability to change circumstances," *not* the inability to help oneself.

Regularly the Church approaches mission as a means of assuming leadership positions over the target group or region. Unfortunately, the stereotypes of the imperialistic missionary and the culturally insensitive Christian worker are all too true. The Church's history in missions work has been commonly marked by insensitivity and inappropriateness.

Unless our ministry among the poor is founded in our personal humility, there can be no fruit. We must minister to the broken out of a posture of brokenness; it is the only way we will be accepted. When we realize that we have as much to learn as we have to offer, true Christlike ministry will freely flow.

The Church must adopt a method of ministry in which she encourages those she ministers among to stand on their own feet. Otherwise, we will continue to nurture an immature and insipid following who can do nothing for themselves. By the Church's misinformed and inappropriate programs and projects, poverty is not only perpetuated, but also created.

Jaykumar Christian, development worker with World Vision India, said, "When we invest our money in the poor, we make the poor into beggars; when we invest in programs for the poor, we turn the poor into beneficiaries; when we invest our life in the poor, the poor will reap life."

5. Forgotten Mission

"We are all called to minister to the poor," writes Viv Grigg in the book *Companion to the Poor*. "Such a ministry is the logical obedience of any disciple imitating the attitudes, character, and teaching of Jesus. He commands everyone to renounce all (Luke 14:33), to give to the poor and live simply."[8]

The key is not only that He focused on the poor, but also that He came. In the story where Jesus healed the man possessed by the legion of demons, the account in Matthew states, "He arrived at the *other side*"

---

8.   Viv Grigg, *Companion to the Poor* (Monrovia, CA: MARC Publications, 1990), 80.

(Mt. 8:28). Jesus got into the boat and went. The mission is that simple. It is a call to go, to make disciples, to baptize, and to teach (see Mt. 28:18-20).

Has the Church forgotten her mission? Has the Church, in her ever-present quest for ease and convenience, altered the final command of her Master? Unless the original mission of her Master is remembered, the poor will go without an example and without a servant. In such a case, there can be no Kingdom community and no holistic development. Thus, the poor will remain in need by the disobedience of the Church.

> *How, then, can they call on the one they have not believed in? And how can they believe in the one of whom they have not heard? And how can they hear without someone preaching to them?* (Romans 10:14)

6. Partiality

The Church of the West readily confesses her love for a lost and dying world, but too often only in word. Indeed, the Church has yet to grapple with the meaning of love for a suffering world. In his book *Rich Christians in an Age of Hunger*, Ron Sider points out, "It is crucial to note that Scripture prescribes justice rather than mere charity."[9]

As a senior at Asbury College in Wilmore, Kentucky, I was beginning to develop a love for the poor, but the Spirit of God was continually purifying my conception of love. One evening before Christmas as I walked into the cafeteria, I saw a sign for "Toys for Tots," a program that makes opportunities available for those in a community to give gifts to the poor and needy. I went up to the table to do my duty and buy a little boy a football for Christmas.

I asked the gentleman seated at the table for a small boy's Christmas wish list. The man informed me that all the children were taken care of; it was their parents whom no one wanted to buy gifts for. I gladly accepted the wish list of a man in the community, a father of three. The only thing this man asked for was a pair of pants, size 32. A pair of pants was all that he wanted, and he couldn't afford them himself.

That evening I sat on my couch and picked up the J. Crew catalogue. I also needed a pair of pants that Christmas and was about to order myself a $44 pair of khaki chinos when I remembered the man's

---

9.   Ronald J. Sider, *Rich Christians in an Age of Hunger* (Dallas, TX: Word Publishing, 1990), 68.

wish list—the poor. I thought, *I can have a friend drive me to Wal-Mart so that I can find this man a $14 pair of generic pants.*

That's when the Spirit convicted me. I was suddenly reminded that when I give to the poor, I am giving to Jesus (see Prov. 19:17). This man was offering me an opportunity to serve Jesus, to buy Jesus a pair of pants for Christmas. And there I was, ready to buy "Jesus" a pair of pants at Wal-Mart and then order myself a pair of pants that cost three times as much!

As soon as I realized what I was doing I was broken. I decided to buy this man the nicest pants I could afford. I opened the opportunity up to my friends and invited them to pitch in if they were willing. As I presented this request, they all responded the same, "Hey, I have a pair of pants that size that I never wear anymore. Should I give him those?"

I began to see how we give to the poor. We figure that the poor don't mind what we give them; they'll take anything. So we give them our leftovers.

What if Jesus came to the door right now? What would He say? "I'm in town for a few days. Do you know where I might be able to find a cheap hotel?" Immediately I would offer Jesus my own bed, insisting that He take it. He then might ask, "I'm hungry. Where might I be able to get a cheap loaf of bread or some soup?" Of course, I would sit the Master down at my own dining table and prepare a feast for Him.

That's how I would treat Jesus. How do I treat the poor? How do I look my brother in the eye and recognize the sufferings of Christ in his poverty?

The teacher of the law confronted Jesus with this very question in Luke 10:25-28. The expert asked Jesus how to obtain eternal life. Jesus tested this man and asked him what he thought the law said. The expert replied, "...'Love the Lord your God with all your heart and with all your soul and with all your strength and with all your mind'; and 'Love your neighbor as yourself.' " Jesus responded, "You have answered correctly. Do this and live" (see Lk. 10:27-28). Our love for the Lord will be seen in our love for our neighbor.

Do we see the child in need, begging on the streets, and automatically want the best education, clothes, food, and housing for that child? Do we see our own children and want the best for them? Do we love the child who begs as we love ourselves and as we love our own children? Or do we show a love based in partiality? How can we love the Lord and not love His children? The poor are "His people" (see Is. 3:15), but do we treat them like that?

Until the Church learns to love her neighbor as herself, her lack of love and lack of compassion will allow her to neglect the needs of the poor.

Jesus came that the poor might receive the good news. The Church, Christ's Body, must be deliberate and intentional in bringing the good news to them. In the second Lausanne statement, the *Manilla Manifesto*, the section on "The Gospel and Social Responsibility" states this:

> "Jesus not only proclaimed the Kingdom of God, he also demonstrated its arrival by works of mercy and power. We are called today to a similar integration of words and deeds. In a spirit of humility we are to preach and teach, minister to the sick, feed the hungry, care for prisoners, help the disadvantaged and handicapped, and deliver the oppressed. While we acknowledge the diversity of spiritual gifts, callings and contexts, we also affirm that good news and good works are inseparable."[10]

Do you remember Prabah and her poverty? Poverty that was partly caused by marginalization. Poverty that was partly caused by a lack of resources. Poverty that was partly caused by an inability to change her circumstances.

Will the Church remain isolated from Prabah? Will the Church continue to be a broken community that Prabah will want no part of? Will the Church continue to hold her resources so tightly that the very things Prabah needs for basic daily survival won't be given to her? Will the Church offer Prabah an imperialistic program with unrealistic demands and handouts only to degrade her and string her out? Will the Church ever go to Prabah? Will the Church love Prabah, even though this poor little girl is dirty and sleeps on a mud floor?

The Church has the answer...if only she will leave her "Majestic Colony" and follow the example of Christ to lift a hand that will alleviate the suffering or Prabah and others.

---

10.   Lausanne Committee for World Evangelism, *Manilla Manifesto* (Manilla, Philippines: July 1989), A,4.

Section III

From Salvation to Wholeness

A former evangelist, missionary, and pastor in Mexico, Mark Nyse-wander is now the pastor of Bethany Missionary Church in Minneapolis, Minnesota. He is also the founder of Threshold Ministries in Wilmore, Kentucky. It is his desire to see the Lord Jesus Christ so honored that Christians become a people who passionately and consistently choose the will of God, who seek His character as well as His ministry, and who display both the power and the purity of the Lord Jesus in the Church. To that end, he urges this generation to turn around and invest in the next generation, so that they might be positioned for the coming harvest.

Chapter 7

Fire and Fullness in the Holy Spirit

by Mark Nysewander

Our God comes and will not be silent; a fire devours before Him, and around Him a tempest rages (Psalm 50:3).

Fire and the Holy Spirit—what is the relationship? It is simply this: You can be filled with the Holy Spirit and know it by the fire-like signs that will flame up in your life. These signs of supernatural fire are similar to the characteristics of natural fire.

Fire-Like Signs

Natural fire brings warmth. When you come into the baptism of the Holy Spirit, things also warm up. Fullness brings a fiery level of experiencing the presence of the Lord Jesus. It is true that you experience Jesus in your salvation. Yet when you enter into the baptism of the Holy Spirit, a greater intensity of the Lord's presence is revealed to you.

E. Stanley Jones, missionary to India, tells of when he experienced the fiery presence of the Lord in his Spirit baptism. Because of the dramatic nature of his experience, it clearly illustrates this burning measure of the Lord's presence. Jones reported, "Suddenly I was filled with a strange refining fire that seemed to course through every portion of my body in cleansing waves." He was introduced to the warmth of a new intimacy with Jesus. The Holy Spirit's fullness warms up your relationship with the Lord.

Natural fire doesn't just bring warmth; it brings light as well. Start a fire and you get instant light. The same is true with Spirit baptism. In Ephesians 1:18 Paul intercedes for the believers. He says, "I pray also that the eyes of your heart may be enlightened...." When you are born again, the eyes of your heart are opened. But when you are filled with the Holy Spirit, the eyes of your heart are enlightened. In other words, God turns up the light.

Paul calls this light "revelation." It is knowledge that comes directly to your human spirit through the Holy Spirit. Enter into the fullness of the Holy Spirit and you become more sensitive to supernatural revelation. Michael Harper, after Spirit baptism, spoke of how this new level of revelation changed his preaching. "I was so clearheaded," he said, "I even had moments when I wanted to stop and listen to what I was saying. It was so interesting!" The light of revelation comes with the Spirit's fullness.

Warmth and light come from fire. But there is another characteristic: energy. Fire creates power. The baptism of the Holy Spirit brings to your life a power to accomplish the will of God and to do Kingdom ministry. In Acts 1:8 Jesus says, "But you will receive power when the Holy Spirit comes on you; and you will be My witnesses in Jerusalem, and in all Judea and Samaria, and to the ends of the earth."

Charles Finney reported an infusion of power that came to his life after being filled with the Holy Spirit. "I immediately found myself endued with such power from on high," he said, "that a few words dropped here and there to individuals were the means of their immediate conversion." The Spirit's power will release gifts in you. These gifts may be different than the gifts Finney received, but the same Spirit will energize your life and ministry.

A supernatural fire of intimacy, revelation, and power flaming up in your life evidences the baptism of the Holy Spirit. As you look at your life and as you look at the life of your church, where is this fire? Maybe you are not seeing any fire. Or it could be you are not experiencing a major flame. So what is the problem?

Three groups of believers do not experience this holy fire of God. Are you in one of these groups? If so, look at the necessary conditions for the fire of the Spirit to flame up in your life.

Light the Fire

Some believers do not see the fire in their lives because they are not filled with the Holy Spirit. Remember that the fire is the evidence of

Spirit baptism. Many do not have the fire because they have never entered into the fullness of the Holy Spirit.

Ignorance is one reason why some believers have never been filled with the Spirit. Maybe you are unaware that there is such an experience as Spirit baptism. You know that you are born again. You know that your sins are forgiven, and you have an assurance that you will go to Heaven when you die. But do you know the infusing work of God that is available to all who believe in Jesus Christ for their salvation?

John the Baptist proclaimed two truths about the ministry of Jesus. First in John 1:29b he said, "Look, the Lamb of God, who takes away the sin of the world!" Through the death and resurrection of Jesus Christ a way has been made for our sins to be forgiven. Also in Matthew 3:11 John said about Jesus, "...He will baptize you with the Holy Spirit and with fire." John proclaimed that Jesus would have a two-pronged ministry. Jesus comes so that you can be born of the spirit, and He comes so that you can be baptized with the Spirit. He wants to save you and then He wants to fill you.

When you believe Jesus for the forgiveness of your sins, the Holy Spirit enters into your dead spirit and begins to minister the benefits of Jesus' blood into your life. You are born again. You experience the joy, peace, and righteousness that come at salvation. This is the ministry of the Holy Spirit within you. You cannot be saved without the ministry of the Holy Spirit in your life. He comes to establish a beachhead of salvation on the shores of your spirit.

But the Spirit of God wants to do more than just establish a beachhead. He wants to launch an all-out invasion! The Holy Spirit desires to invade every area of your life with His presence and power. This is what it means to be filled with the Holy Spirit. You open up your life to the Spirit of God and invite Him to fill your mind, will, and emotions with His purpose and power.

If you have never intentionally asked God to fill you with the Holy Spirit, seek Him for this invasion of holiness and power. In Luke 11:13 Jesus said, "If you then, though you are evil, know how to give good gifts to your children, how much more will your Father in heaven give the Holy Spirit to those who ask Him!" Let this be an invitation to ask Him. Ask Him to fill you with the Holy Spirit. Be as intentional in your faith for Spirit baptism as you are for your salvation.

If you are not ready to ask for this invasion of the Holy Spirit, at least ask God to make you hungry for this work. Spirit baptism is not an option.

It is the purpose of God for every believer. In Acts 1:4 Jesus Himself said that it was the promise of the Father. Now is the time to go for fullness.

The Fear of Fire

Other believers are not ignorant of this work of God. They have heard about it. But they still do not seek life in the Spirit because they fear the Holy Spirit. It is fear more than ignorance that keeps them from fullness. Maybe this is the reason that there is no fire in your life. You are thinking, *I know persons who claim to be filled with the Spirit and they do a lot of daffy and hurtful things. I'm trying to live a sane life and I'm afraid of doing anything weird.*

It's true that there are believers filled with the Holy Spirit who do some stupid things. But there is a reason for this kind of behavior. When you open your life to the Holy Spirit's fullness, you open up to the supernatural world. You want to hear and obey every word the Holy Spirit speaks into your life. The supernatural world is the world of the Holy Spirit. But not everything in the supernatural world is the Holy Spirit. It is possible to open up to the supernatural world and be deceived by an unclean spirit. It is also possible to do things out of self-interest. That is why it is so important that a Spirit-filled believer get into the Word of God and walk with other Spirit-filled believers in this new life of power and holiness. You must walk in discernment.

There are Spirit-filled believers who walk without discernment, the Word of God, or accountability. They become easily deceived by the voice of the enemy or their flesh and end up doing some stupid things. Such a group of undiscerning believers were creating problems several years ago in a church. When concerned church members approached the pastor, they asked, "Do you think that these folks will make it to Heaven?" The pastor responded, "They will make it to Heaven if they don't overshoot it!" The person who is Spirit baptized without discernment and accountability many times will overshoot the will of God and misuse the fire.

People also misuse natural fire. They burn down homes and forests or burn themselves. But do you stop using natural fire because people misuse it? Of course you don't. Our regular, daily lives would be impossible without natural fire.

Even though people have misused the fire of the Spirit and have done some foolish things, don't fear the Holy Spirit. You can't live fully as a believer without this divine fire. Yes, it is dangerous to be filled with the Holy Spirit, but it is much more dangerous not to be filled. You must have the fire of God!

Repent of any fear of the Holy Spirit. How can you fear the One who puts in you the very benefits of the blood of Jesus? Ask God to fill you. Then get into the Word of God and get around other Spirit-filled believers. The best way to enter into Pentecost is to go together. Seek the Holy Spirit's fullness and seek discernment to walk in the Spirit.

Doubting the Fire

Why is there no supernatural fire of the Spirit? Some are not filled because of ignorance and fear. Still others, even though they are filled, don't see the fire because they don't continue in faith. Maybe you have asked the Lord to fill you with the Holy Spirit and He has. You have even seen some signs of His deeper activity in your life. But you still don't see mighty flames of the Holy Spirit. Because there is no immediate or dramatic signs of fullness, you now doubt that God can do in you what He promised to do by His Holy Spirit.

This seemed to be the problem with Timothy. He was filled, but he had doubts about the mighty flames of God in his own life. Timothy followed Paul around Asia Minor and saw in Paul the characteristics of supernatural fire. He witnessed in Paul a fiery intimacy with Jesus, clear revelations from the Spirit, and demonstrations of power in ministry. When Timothy looked at his own life, he didn't see the same signs. He doubted that the Spirit could flame up in him like he had seen in Paul.

I remember a time when I lived in doubt over these manifestations of the Holy Spirit in my life. Having sought the Lord for the baptism of the Holy Spirit, I was sure that He had filled me. The Holy Spirit had accomplished significant plate shifts in my life. It was a sign of His deep working. But I did not immediately see the mighty flames of revelation, intimacy, and power that I had expected. I concluded that I was a second-class, Spirit-filled believer. Not expecting God to do in me what He had promised, I soon settled into a life of doubt. I was in such doubt that when God did work in me, I would explain it away as "coincidence," "emotions," or a "funny thought." I was convinced that there was nothing more for me. I was filled, but I had quit believing for the signs of His fullness.

If this is your condition, look at what Paul writes in Second Timothy 1:6-7. In this passage, Paul warns Timothy of spiritual timidity. When you are naturally timid, you don't have any confidence in yourself. When you are spiritually timid, you don't have confidence in the Holy Spirit. Paul tells Timothy that he is filled with the Holy Spirit. He reminds Timothy that he was present when they laid hands on Timothy and prayed for him. The fire of God was within him. Paul encouraged him to fan the flame until he had the mighty manifestations of the Spirit in his life.

Here is a word for you. If you have been filled with the Holy Spirit but are not seeing the flames of God, you must fan the flame that is in you. Yet how do you fan the flame of the Spirit?

Fan the Flame

First, fan the flame with faith. You need to believe that the Holy Spirit can do in you what He says that He can do in you. You will never see the fire of the Spirit flame up in your life unless you first believe that He can flame up. Maybe you thought that the baptism of the Holy Spirit was the end of faith. Well, it's not. In reality it is the beginning. Now is the time to believe like never before. Believe for greater manifestations of the Lord's presence, power, and revelation.

Smith Wigglesworth, the great Pentecostal evangelist, once said that he would rather minister with someone who wasn't filled with the Holy Spirit but was believing God for something, than to minister with someone who was filled with the Holy Spirit and wasn't believing God for anything. Faith doesn't end with fullness. What do you believe God for now? What is the next frontier of faith that you will cross in the Spirit? Fan the fire with faith.

Second, fan the flame by putting yourself in the places where the fire will flame up in your life. Do you want greater intimacy with Jesus Christ? Give time to Him in both public and private worship. Learn new dimensions of expressing your affections to Him. As you do this, the fire of spiritual passion will ignite in your heart.

Seek the voice of God. If you want revelation, then go after His voice. Get into His Word. Fast and pray until you hear the whispers of the Spirit. As you put yourself in a place to hear Him, revelation will come.

Do you desire greater flames of the Spirit's power? Get into situations of ministry where God has to show up or you are in a lot of trouble. Risk for the sake of the Kingdom. Pray for the sick. Come against the power of the enemy. Share the gospel. As you give yourself to intimacy, revelation, and power, you will see ever-increasing levels of the fire of God in your life. Fan the flame by going after these expressions of His fire.

Repent of your doubt and get back into faith. The fire is in you through the fullness of the Holy Spirit. Now fan the flame and watch the fire blaze up in your life.

A Burning Sacrifice

There is another reason why believers don't see the fire of the Holy Spirit. Maybe you asked the Spirit of God to fill you and even saw signs of the fire in your life. Now you no longer see the fire. Why? You don't see it because you quenched the work of the Holy Spirit—the fire is out.

Maybe you're thinking, *Why would I put out the fire of God once it has been lit?* You put it out because you do not like what the Spirit is doing in your life. It is important that you understand why God fills us with the Holy Spirit. If you don't understand this, you can work against the Holy Spirit's activity in your life. Some people seek the baptism of the Holy Spirit because they only want a good case of goose bumps. But this isn't the purpose of God in filling us with the Holy Spirit. The experience may come wrapped in power, but drama is not the reason for Spirit baptism.

God wants to fill you with the Holy Spirit because He wants to make you a burning sacrifice completely consumed by fire. Hebrews 12:29 says, "Our God is a consuming fire." He will consume anything in your life that keeps you from Him. God wants you holy.

Several years ago I was in a conference in California. John Wimber was leading the service. He invited all the people in ministry to come forward for a prayer of impartation over our ministries. In the middle of the prayer he called out to God, "Let Your fire fall, now." Immediately in my mind I could see this firestorm burning in front of me, behind me, and around me. It was an awesome blaze burning out of control. For the first time, I saw a vision of the Holy Spirit's engulfing presence. Up to that time when I thought of the Holy Spirit, I imagined a little pilot light in the basement of my soul. I saw Him as only a flickering little flame.

But the Spirit of God is a mighty firestorm. He burns wherever He desires. He will blaze up in your life to burn up or melt anything that stands against the holiness of the Lord.

Surrender to the Fire

This is the reason why total consecration is the condition for correct entry into the fullness of the Holy Spirit. *Consecration* means that you give the Holy Spirit the freedom to direct and change your life. You are saying to the Spirit, "Move into any area and transform it as You desire." If you don't make that kind of consecration in the beginning of your Spirit-filled life, sooner or later you will be faced with another hard decision. You will have to decide if the Holy Spirit can burn into guarded areas of your life or if you will quench His work. He is an engulfing flame who wants to make you a sacrifice completely consumed by His holy fire.

I was once in a meeting where a fellow pastor sought the Lord for the fullness of the Holy Spirit. God came in supernatural force and radically touched his life. Months later, I saw him again. He informed me that some of his friends and denominational leaders had talked to him. They told him that if the word got out among the denominational churches that he was filled with the Spirit, it would ruin his career as a pastor. People would think he was too fanatical. He then looked at me and said, "For that reason I have decided to give up this Spirit-filled stuff."

At least he was honest! I know some folks who have quenched the Spirit and continue acting like they still have the fire of God. Here was this pastor's problem. He invited the Holy Spirit to come in fullness. The Lord answered his prayer. But when the blaze of God began to melt his reputation and burn up his security, this young pastor said, "That's enough!" He wasn't willing to give the firestorm freedom to burn through his life.

It is costly to be filled with the Holy Spirit. The fire of holiness will touch areas of your life that are difficult to give up. But there is a reason for this baptism of fire. In Second Chronicles 7, you will find the story of Solomon's dedication of the temple. After Solomon prays the prayer of dedication, verse 1 says that "...fire came down from heaven and consumed the burnt offering and the sacrifices, and the glory of the Lord filled the temple." The fire of God fell and consumed the sacrifices on the altar, then the manifest presence of the living God filled the temple.

God sent a baptism of fire so that He could send a baptism of His glory. Give His Spirit freedom to burn throughout your life so that He can fill you with His manifest presence. Psalm 50:3 declares, "Our God comes and will not be silent; a fire devours before Him, and around Him a tempest rages." The baptism of the Holy Spirit is the firestorm that prepares for the coming of the Lord's presence. It is the outer sparks of the white heat of His glory.

If you have been resisting the fiery ministry of the Holy Spirit in your life, repent of quenching His work. Welcome His engulfing blaze, and you welcome the glory of the living God.

Maybe you have been wrestling with God over full surrender to His purpose in you life. Perhaps there is an area of your life that you just can't give up to God. What can you do? F.B. Meyer, the great Baptist preacher, was at a point in his life where he too was wrestling over total surrender to be filled with the Holy Spirit. There was an area he wasn't willing to surrender to the blaze of the Spirit. Finally, Meyer prayed a simple prayer like this, "Lord, I'm not willing, but I'm willing for You to make me willing." God could work with that! The Lord changed the desires of Meyer's heart, and he was filled with the Holy Spirit.

Do you need to pray that prayer? It is a very dangerous prayer because God *will* bring you to a place of willingness. Don't quench the fire of the Spirit. Let Him have His way in your life no matter the cost.

The Firestorm That Makes You Holy

In Ezekiel 36:27 God promises, "I will put My Spirit in you and move you to follow My decrees and be careful to keep My laws." The fire of God residing in you transforms your human will and takes away your bent toward selfishness. You begin to do the will of God, even when you have to choose against your own selfish desires.

How does this firestorm move you to do God's will? In the full blaze of His presence, the Holy Spirit so infuses you with His nature that you start to choose passionately and consistently for God. The early Church fathers had a popular illustration for this work of infusion. A sword by its very nature is cold, hard steel. But if you put the sword in a fire and leave it there long enough, the nature of the sword will change. It soon becomes glowing and hot, just like the fire. The sword doesn't become the fire; it simply takes on the nature of the fire.

When you surrender totally to the firestorm of the Spirit and stay daily in His work, He infuses you with His nature. Holiness comes from the Spirit who is holy. You don't become the Holy Spirit, but you take on His holy nature through full and constant exposure to His fiery presence. The Holy Spirit reproduces in your unique personality the very character of the Lord Jesus Christ.

Your holy destiny as a believer is in the fire of the Spirit. If the fire has not been lit, seek for the baptism of the Holy Spirit. If the fire has been released in fullness, believe every day for a new dimension of the Lord's presence, revelation, and power. And at any cost, do not quench the fire of God that is raging through your life. You can trust His ways, for they are always to make you holy.

Dr. Carlos Mraida is co-pastor with Dr. Pablo Deiros of the Central Baptist Church of Buenos Aires, Argentina. He holds a master's degree from the International Baptist Theological Seminary in Buenos Aires and a doctorate from the Catholic University of Argentina. Dr. Mraida has also co-authored with Dr. Deiros Latinoamerica en Llamas (Latin America in Flames).

Chapter 8

Inner Healing to Live in Freedom

by Dr. Carlos Mraida

Holiness has a double dimension: the dimension of *separation* and the dimension of *consecration*. We are sanctified—that is, separated and placed apart—from evil. Yet in sanctification we are also consecrated and dedicated for what is good. To forget about this double dimension is very dangerous. When we only understand sanctification as separation, we diminish its significance and limit it to a list of things that the Christian must not do. The result of this perspective is to form "Christian ghettos," which are separate from the world but neither affect nor transform it. But to the contrary, to consider holiness just as consecration leads us to form a legion of activists lacking the character to back their deeds. They try to change the world, but they fail to achieve their objective because they forget that the message is the messenger. From the biblical perspective a choice cannot be made between both dimensions. It is not possible to choose between purity and power. The three times holy God desires a complete holiness for us (see Rev. 4:8).

Both dimensions require clear and powerful encounters with the Lord. It is impossible to experience a radical separation from evil, as God wants, without an outpouring of His powerful grace. It is useless to try to be salt, light, or leaven that changes people's lives and the sinful structures of society without the *dunamis* of the Spirit. This outpouring of power that separates and consecrates begins in the moment of conversion, is renewed, and grows permanently, especially through profound experiences of encountering the Lord. In other words, there is an initial experience *and* a continuous process of sanctification. There are diverse new experiences of power that push and accelerate the progress. As a result, we face a double dimension of life, *separation* and *consecration*, and a double dimension in time, *experience* and *process*.

When we understand this double life-and-time dynamic, we begin to understand that inner healing is essential for our sanctification. We cannot live fully in holiness without being healthy.

Inner Healing and Holiness as Separation

It is impossible to move ahead in our separation from evil without inner healing. Why? Because sin is nothing more than *accumulated frustration that we try to resolve in ways contrary to the will of God*. For example, a woman who has not had a good relationship with her father—a relationship which should have taught her that she is loved and valued—may seek affirmation in numerous sexual relationships with different men. Such a woman is seeking for the father she never had. Similarly, the man who was raised in extreme poverty may seek to resolve that sense of destitution and thereby develop an extremely ambitious and greedy personality. A believer who has had a hard and violent father will often have a bad image of authority in his mind and will probably go from congregation to congregation because of an inability to submit. A daughter of God who from childhood felt as if she never measured up to her sister may become the instigator of constant confrontations and divisions in her local church. These are just a few illustrations of the ways in which sin is unresolved frustration seeking to satisfy itself in the wrong ways.

All these situations come to our attention as sins, such as fornication, unrestrained ambition, greed, lack of submission, or a spirit of division. What we often end up doing is implementing disciplinary measures for those who fall into these sins. We read the appropriate biblical demands. We give them some counsel to not fall into the same sin again. We warn them about the risks they are running. We pray for them. And we apply some kind of punitive ecclesiastical measure to them. We do all this to show them the demands of holiness and to help them to live out the demands. Yet we are only working with the manifestation of the problem.

The result of this kind of pastoral approach is that the people continue to fall into the same sin all over again. Even in the best of cases, though they will stop committing those sins, they will end up seeking to resolve their frustration through other sinful means. We have worked with the consequences of the problem, the sin, but we have not addressed the causes. We are asking for purity from the people without healing their wounds. To demand holiness without healing is to push people into guilt and frustration. Therefore, it is necessary to have those encounters with the healing power of the Lord in order to live in holiness. The result is that these basic needs or wants in our personality are resolved by means of the healing grace of God and never again through sinful means.

Confession of sins, an indispensable element for sanctification, is not that moment in which we finally change God's mind and convince Him to forgive us. Rather, it is the moment in which *our* minds are changed so that we clearly see our need and accept God's forgiveness. That is healing. Saint Augustine said that we must hate the sin and love the sinner. Holiness is not only hating the sin, but also loving the sinner in me. I need to love me enough to seek to heal my past in such a way that I will stop repeating the same mistakes and stop hurting myself. The great men of God were great saints when they saw themselves as great sinners who needed healing. The test of knowing how holy I am in my life is not how close I feel to God according to my conduct, but rather how aware I am of my need for Him.

We call inner healing a "therapeutic spiritual encounter between someone and God through which the person receives healing for his past wounds." All of us have suffered in some moment of our lives. Some people have experienced suffering because of *want*, because of emotional, physical, or material needs that weren't met. Others have suffered because of *traumatic experiences*, such as the death of a loved one, an accident, great danger, rape, or other abuse, etc. Others have experienced wounds provoked by pain in *interpersonal relationships*. And all of us have suffered as a result of *our own sins* and poor decisions.

Thus, we have four principal sources of suffering. If we don't experience the healing of these past wounds, these sources of suffering from the past are converted into sources of frustration for the present, and the sources of present frustration are transformed into sources of future sinfulness. Holiness, when understood in its first dimension (separation from evil), implies deactivating the causes that provoke the frustration and sin. We must not only be cleansed from sins but also from the basis of sin. In inner healing we confront the person with the love and power of God. A whole or healthy person is one who, having accepted the love of God, accepts himself and offers acceptance to others. Of course this does not immediately translate into greater holiness, for that depends on the voluntary desire of the person. But what I am saying is that as we experience inner healing, we find freedom from old strongholds that previously impeded our living as God desires and that once compulsively pushed us to sin. In having an encounter with this healing power, the believer experiences the disappearance of the compulsion and is now free to *decide* whether or not to live in holiness.

Inner Healing and Holiness as Consecration

Holiness is not just about what is evil and old; it is also about what is good and what is future. In this dimension we appreciate holiness as consecration. We are sanctified—separated from evil—but we are also set apart and dedicated to good. If the sanctifying purpose of God was strictly to separate us from evil, we would already be in Heaven. We would be completely separated from this world and from the state of things contrary to the will of God, which are inescapable in this earthly reality. But this is not what God wants. God left us in the world with the purpose of being a holy nation, to proclaim the praises of Him who called us from darkness to His marvelous light (see 1 Pet. 2:9 KJV). We have a mission to accomplish, and we have been sanctified and consecrated to that mission.

If we don't minister inner healing to people who desire to live in holiness and are consecrating their lives to serve the Lord, we will notice that these people find themselves in bondage to old things, things that don't permit them to fully develop their ministries and gifts. Unhealed wounds from the past will hold them back from entering into and developing consecration to God. For example, a pastor may be completely consecrated to the Lord, working and straining to win people to Christ. God moves, and many people are incorporated into the membership of that pastor's church. But it generally won't take long before the unhealed wounds in the life of that pastor will begin to manifest themselves through hard attitudes toward those people, and one day, the people begin to leave. The pastor will enter a crisis of discouragement that causes the level of his consecration to diminish. The evangelist who never felt valued nor received recognition from his parents during his formative years may become raised up and anointed by God with a powerful ministry with signs and wonders. One day he finds that the flow seems to be blocked. He doesn't realize that lately he has been trying to heal his need for approval through his work on the platform, making himself the center of attention instead of giving the glory to God. An intercessor consecrated to spiritual warfare may suddenly have to abandon the battle because the devil penetrated her rearguard and destroyed her marriage—all because there were unresolved issues in her own interior.

Sanctification as consecration requires an encounter of power through which we are filled with the anointing of the Holy Spirit. Suddenly we are invested with power to minister, to preach the good news to the poor, to heal the brokenhearted, to free the prisoners, to give sight to the blind, and to announce the year of the Lord's favor (see Lk. 4:18-19). Yet in order for this to happen we need to experience that encounter, after which we can say, "The Spirit of the Lord is on me because He has anointed me." But for that to happen, and above all to have its marvelous effects remain, healing is *necessary*. It is just as is shown in the anecdote of that man who prayed and cried, "Lord, fill me with Your Spirit, fill me with Your Spirit, fill me." His wife, hearing the prayer of her husband, quickly added, "Lord, before You fill him, plug the holes first." Behind this cute story is hidden a great truth concerning the holes in our lives that need to be "plugged" or healed if we want to live filled with the Spirit and to be a blessing for the world.

Inner Healing and Holiness as an Experience

In addition to a double dimension of life, holiness implies a double dimension in time. Holiness is manifested as a specific experience, but it also is shown as a series of experiences that add new branches of growth to our initial experience with Christ. This means that we *were* sanctified and *are being* sanctified. Saint Paul expresses this tension between the event and the process well as he greets the church in Corinth in his first letter, "To the church of God in Corinth, to those *sanctified* in Christ Jesus and *called to be holy*..." (1 Cor. 1:2). Paul was stating that they had already been sanctified in Christ Jesus in their initial experience, but they were now called to be holy each day.

When we forget either of the two temporal dimensions, we lose sight of the fullness of the work of the Holy Spirit. If we accept the process of sanctification but forget the experience or experiences, we run the risk of seeing this process as almost imperceptible human progress where the miraculous or supernatural has almost no space to break into the life of the believer. The reality is that without this initial experience, there is no process of sanctification. And without experiencing the power throughout the process, either a blockage will occur or one will see only very slow growth. These concrete experiences of powerfully encountering God that shake and move us in holiness, push us to grow in separation and consecration. Some of these concrete experiences of power, leading us to greater holiness, are the inner healing experiences.

Just as in holiness, inner healing can also manifest itself as a concrete experience and as a process. There are times that, as happens in physical healing, we pray for a person for healing of memories, for healing of wounds and negative feelings, or for the etching of new mental images, and the person immediately receives healing from God. The person feels a great release and great joy. He or she will exclaim, "I feel like the great weight I was carrying is gone!" Having experienced such a clear demonstration of God's love leads to a renewal of love and devotion to the Lord. These persons can testify, "I was healed."

Nevertheless, in the measure that they continue to grow in their commitment with the Lord and that the Spirit leads them into new experiences, they will receive light on hidden levels of new things in their lives that need to be healed. Some are healed by the Lord in that same moment of revelation. Others need a process of ministry and healing that is more prolonged. If they only have the healing experienced at one point in time in their past, these other areas of their lives that have been shown to need healing will become sources of frustration and sin and will be impediments to greater holiness. Just as with holiness, that person has been healed and called to be whole.

Inner Healing and Holiness as a Process

When we only receive sanctification as a concrete experience and lose sight of the process of sanctification, we begin to develop attitudes of self-sufficiency. We lose sight of the fact that this experience acts as our starting point of living life daily with God and having other special experiences of power, which are repeated under the same conditions as in our experience of conversion. When we come to Christ, we show ourselves just as we are—in need of His mercy and His grace. We recognize that we are unable to do anything by ourselves for our salvation. In that way we are born again, and we begin the process of sanctification. But after we become children of God, we often decide to change the divine methodology. Instead of coming near to God for our growth in holiness as we did at the beginning (which is to say, as needy sinners), we start planning how to try hard enough to not sin without God's help.

This perspective of sanctification as a unique and specific event, instead of a prolonged process that includes additional experiences of power, leads us also to a poor understanding of our personal situation as believers. Many good believers say, "I don't need inner healing, because I already received everything from God in my conversion experience [or, "in my experience of being baptized with the Holy Spirit," or, "in my sanctification experience"]. I am already a new creature; all the old things have passed away." Nevertheless, this affirmation enters into two serious errors. The first is that these believers' lives don't demonstrate that all the old things passed away. The second is that the Bible doesn't teach that. What the Word of God says is that if anyone is in Christ, he is a new creature. The old things are passing away, and behold, all things are "being made new" (see 2 Cor. 5:17 KJV). This shows us that there is a *process* that begins with a specific experience and is deepened by new experiences and power encounters in which the love and healing of God are manifested in our lives.

Inner Healing and Holiness as Parallel Transformations

In both actions of the power of God there is a powerful spiritual experience that initiates sanctification as well as inner healing. Starting from that specific experience, a sanctification and healing process begins that includes similar elements. The initial experience is followed by illumination. The Holy Spirit suddenly shows us areas in our lives that need to be sanctified—actions, motivations, relationships, thoughts, etc. In the same way He reveals that there are things in our lives that belong to the past but continue to condition our present and, therefore, need to be healed. These things would include memories, images, commands, feelings, etc.

The next step in the process is to renounce. We confess our sins in prayer. We acknowledge our failures, and we repent and renounce them. The same thing happens with inner healing. We renounce those bondages from the past in such a way that they no longer hold our present in bondage. The renouncing is vital in both processes because it is here that the devil loses legal authority over our lives. Upon our confessing sins, he no longer has anything to grab a hold of to accuse us. When we renounce things from the past, he loses what he needs to impede our growth and health. Since satan is not omniscient, he cannot read our thoughts. So we must renounce in an audible voice. That way the adversary and accuser is notified of our decisions and loses his rights over us.

The sanctification and healing process continues by *asking* God for both forgiveness and healing. This is where the power of the Holy Spirit is manifested to cleanse our lives and restore us for greater holiness. This experience of encountering the God of holiness and healing can be dramatic or not, spectacular or not. But it is inevitable that having an encounter with God will be a powerful, transforming experience.

After this, the challenge is to live in holiness and health. As long as we do that, the Holy Spirit will continue to do His job of revelation, to show us new things that we need to clean and new things that we need to heal to be more holy; that is, to be more like Christ. In this way the process is repeated. However, it is not a cycle where we return to where we were before; rather, it is a process of constant growth.

Inner Healing and Holiness in Your Life

So that the reading of this book would not be merely an intellectual exercise, I encourage you to go through the following steps for your own inner healing. I have led thousands of people around the world through these steps of prayer, and God's power healed their hearts. He will do the same for you.

1. Ask the Holy Spirit to take control of your life.
2. Ask the Holy Spirit to reveal wounds that still affect you.
3. In an audible voice, renounce the negative feelings of hate, resentment, bitterness, and fear. Renounce also the images, demands, words, and memories that hurt you.
4. Forgive, in the name of Jesus, those who have hurt you and bless them.
5. Ask the Holy Spirit to search your heart to reveal any unconfessed sin.
6. Ask for forgiveness of your sins and repent sincerely.
7. Submit your life to the Lordship of Christ.
8. Ask and receive in faith healing for your heart.
9. Ask and receive in faith a healing touch of the Holy Spirit.
10. Read this prayer out loud that I now pray for you:

    "Father, in the name of Jesus, I release my brother/sister's life from every bondage and I break every yoke in his/her life. Breathe upon him/her the fullness of the Holy Spirit. Amen."

Jehovah, the Holy One of Israel (see Is. 43:3), is the same God who calls Himself Jehovah your healer (see Ex. 15:26). The same God who challenges us to "be holy as He is holy" (see 1 Pet. 1:16), also lovingly asks us, "Do you want to be healed?" (see Jn. 5:6) May your response be, "Yes, Lord, I want to be holy and healthy."

Dr. Pablo Deiros is co-pastor of Central Baptist Church in Buenos Aires, Argentina, the oldest Baptist church in that nation, with about 2,000 members. He holds a number of masters degrees in history and Church history, and a Ph.D. in history from Southwestern Baptist Theological Seminary in the United States. A professor of Church history for 25 years at the International Baptist Theological Seminary in Buenos Aires, he also is a visiting professor at many colleges and seminaries in several countries, including Princeton Theological Seminary and Fuller Theological Seminary in the United States. He is co-author along with Dr. Carlos Mraida of Latinoamerica en Llamas (Latin America in Flames)*.*

Pablo Bottari was a barber in Buenos Aires before he became the Director of Deliverance Ministry for evangelist Carlos Annacondia. For 12 years he supervised the activities in the deliverance tent at the campaigns, and he has personally participated in the deliverances of more than 60,000 individuals. Today he serves on the pastoral staff of Central Baptist Church in Buenos Aires, Argentina, and is more and more in demand as an international teacher on deliverance in the local churches.

Chapter 9

Deliverance From Dark Strongholds

by Dr. Pablo Deiros and Pablo Bottari

My (Dr. Pablo Deiros) first experience with inner healing and deliverance began when an 18-year-old woman oppressed by a demon almost destroyed my office at the Central Baptist Church in Buenos Aires, Argentina. At that time I knew of no one who could handle such a situation. My church and I quickly began to learn how to minister to those troubled with demonic oppression.

There is an enormous need for inner healing and deliverance, not only in my home country but also in every country that I have visited. Unfortunately, this is a ministry that has been neglected by the Church for many decades.

In Argentina, evangelist Carlos Annacondia has a 150-foot deliverance tent with yellow and white stripes. It is set aside exclusively for ministering to those at the crusade in whom demons manifest through shaking, falling, screaming, or some other very observable way. When Annacondia begins to rebuke satan at a crusade, a powerful electricity goes through the people. It is simply an incredible work of the Holy Spirit. At his crusades a constant stream of people, often hundreds of them, go into that deliverance tent every night. Practically all of them come out with a substantial degree of healing and deliverance.

For many years Pablo Bottari supervised the deliverance tent at Annacondia's crusades where hundreds of old and new believers have been liberated from demonic oppression. With the help of the Holy Spirit, he developed a deliverance model that is quiet, loving, dignified, and very effective. It is pastoral and teachable.

After my experience with the woman in my office, I learned about the ministry of Bottari and his ten-step model of deliverance, which we now follow at Central Baptist Church.

I have personally tried several other methods of deliverance. We like Bottari's model because it is pastoral, not spectacular; it goes to the root of a problem rather than dealing only with the symptom; and you can see, right on the spot, the freedom, joy, and peace on the face of the person ministered to.

The need for inner healing and deliverance is so prevalent that we have trained most of the members of our church in Bottari's model. It is now a normal part of our church life.

At a crusade in our church with Annacondia a few years ago, we had 1,300 professions of faith, and 700—more than half of these—went through our deliverance tent. We also see many deliverances at other times.

Deliverance is not only a ministry to the new believer. We have found in Argentina and other countries a great need for this help on the part of believers of many years, including pastors and church leaders. Until very recently, no one has been helping in this area. I have personally seen hundreds and hundreds of pastors who needed help. They knew that their ministry was severely impeded by demonic oppression, but they did not know help was available. In one country, I know of a region where more than 75 percent of the pastors and pastors' wives carry heavy burdens requiring inner healing and deliverance because of just one problem— traumatic sexual experiences as children.

One of the things we do now is hold clinics just for pastors and leaders. We call them clinics because their purpose is to help liberate pastors and leaders. One way to handle this is to have a small crusade with two deliverance tents. One tent is set aside for pastors and leaders to receive training and go through deliverance themselves. The second is for people who manifest during the crusade. The pastors and leaders can then go work in the second tent to get practical training. We are learning and changing our clinics from year to year.[1]

---

1.   Dr. Deiros, Dr. Mraida, and Pastor Bottari have worked with Randy Clark in the United States in conferences and clinics. For future updates, call the office of Global Awakening at (314) 416-9239.

The Church needs to be purified as the prospective Bride of Christ, and God will not start with the sheep. He will start with the leaders of the Church. A healed leader, a freed leader, will bring freedom, deliverance, peace, and health to the rest of the congregation. That is why we organize these clinics, and the pastors come by the hundreds. They are hungry. They are saying, "At last someone is paying attention to the things that have been hurting me, binding me, and preventing me from serving my church the way God wants me to serve."

My brothers and sisters in the United States tend to think that they must go overseas to see demonic forces at work. That is a lie. I have worked with mission boards and denominations in North America, and *I have seen more demonic work in believers in the United States than anywhere else in the world.* The reason we don't see much manifestation in the United States is that the devil is very comfortable in our churches and we have not bothered him. If we begin to take the devil seriously, rebuke him, and denounce him by name, we will find him in our church members and leaders. We have had much teaching on evangelizing and discipling in this country, but very little on inner healing and deliverance.

What follows next in this chapter is the wonderful model that my colleague and friend Pablo Bottari has developed to set men and women free from demonic strongholds.

A Deliverance Ministry Model

Whenever I (Pablo Bottari) approach the ministry of deliverance, I assume that the demonic oppression gained entrance through an "open door," such as a hurtful relationship, a traumatic event, a prolonged illness, or a habitual sin. I have discovered that if all open doors are not "closed," a deliverance is often difficult, sometimes humiliating, and may be only temporary. On the other hand, if all open doors are closed, the actual deliverance is usually easy, quick, not humiliating, and more likely to be permanent. (In this chapter, I will use the term *prayee* to refer to those receiving deliverance. I will also be using masculine pronouns. Please know that it is intended to refer to both men and women.)

This model is suitable for crusade settings where a demonic presence may be manifested by shaking, falling, and perhaps screaming, yet it is also appropriate for use in local church or private settings where a believer asks for help to set him free from a compulsive emotional or behavior problem and where obvious demonic manifestations are not usually encountered. In providing help to believers needing liberation and inner healing, there are several principles that the minister should keep in mind. At the same time, we must resist the temptation to take these steps as a mechanical "how to" kind of thing.

Principles for Deliverance

- Deliverance ministry should be guided by God's love and by a dependence on the Holy Spirit every step of the way. Remember, your main job is not to cast out a demon; it is to help a soul whom the Lord loves and does not want to hurt. Behind this entire ministry there must be the heart of God for a suffering soul whom the devil is oppressing. Don't ever treat the person being ministered to like a demon!
- Most likely, the prayee is a very hurt person. Don't hesitate to interrupt the ten-step model to lovingly pray in a general way, or better, in a specific way, for the healing of his wounds and hurts. This may be needed more than once during the ministry.
- The power to heal and deliver is in the name of Jesus. You cannot use His name too much!

Ten Steps to Freedom

Step 1:   Give the individual priority.

Be loving, not militant. Firmness is necessary in bringing a demon under Christ's authority, but the prayee himself needs to feel loved, accepted, and encouraged. The prayee may have been in bondage for years and has perhaps received prayers that did more harm than good. Encourage him; he is on his way to freedom!

Step 2:   If a spirit manifests, bring it under submission, in the name of Jesus.

Take authority over any spirit that manifests and make it be quiet. Simply say something like, "Submit, in the name of Jesus!" or "Be quiet, in Jesus' name! I want to talk to (Bruce or Helen)." Keep repeating such commands until the spirit is quiet. Don't be surprised if this takes time. Be persistent. It is helpful to tell the prayee you are talking to the demon that is manifesting and not to him.

Ask others not to touch or speak to the prayee or pray loudly while you are quieting a demon. Spirits are very quick to sense divided authority. If others impinge on your authority, it is more difficult to quiet the demon.

Step 3: Establish and maintain communication with the prayee.

The prayee's cooperation is essential for deliverance and inner healing. He must help you find the "open doors" and get them closed. This means that you must be able to talk with him. You can't do this if a spirit is manifesting.

Maintaining communication during ministry may require additional commands to spirits to submit. The prayee perhaps cannot hold his head up, look at you, or sit still. If necessary, order the spirits again to submit. This may take time, but it is absolutely necessary. Don't speak to any spirit except to give it orders, in the name of Jesus.

Step 4: Ask the prayee what he wants to be freed from and try to make sure he really does want to get free.

Unless God sovereignly intervenes, it is probably impossible to permanently liberate a person unless he genuinely wants to be free. Successful deliverance requires unqualified forgiveness, sincere repentance, and renunciation of wrong conduct and attitudes. It requires willingness to change any lifestyle that gave entrance to the demon in the first place. If the prayee seeks deliverance without these, he is likely to soon again be in bondage, even if a deliverance is "successful."

If you find that the prayee is not a candidate for deliverance for any reason, don't be offended. Pray for him and bless him, but don't pray for his deliverance. Encourage him to come back later for deliverance help if he really wishes to become free.

Step 5: Make sure that the prayee has accepted Jesus as his Savior and Lord.

The prayee will need the help of the Holy Spirit to stay free. This should be explained to him. If he is not a believer, perhaps you can lead him to Christ. If you cannot, pray for him; pray for his healing; but do not pray for liberation. Encourage him to take the step of making Jesus his Lord and then return for deliverance and healing.

Go on to the following steps only if the prayee really wants to get free and only if he has received Jesus as the Lord of his life.

Step 6:   Interview the prayee to discover the event or events, the conduct, or the relationship situations that have led to his bondage or bondages.

The purpose of the interview is to expose the places where forgiveness is required, where healing is needed, and where repentance and breaking of bondages is needed. These places are the open doors.

If there is a specific bondage the person wants to be free from, start there. If there is no obvious other place to start, begin with his relationship with his father and with his mother. Then continue on through other relationships and then through other areas. Look for places where the prayee has been mistreated or hurt and for ways that the prayee himself has sinned. The more thorough the interview and the more detailed the forgiveness and repentance are, the better.

Interviewing by "areas" is a convenient way to make sure the interview is thorough. The minister should cover one area fully, then go on to another.

Areas include the following: relationships (father, mother, etc.), drugs, the occult, sex outside of marriage, trauma, curses, habitual sins, as well as miscellaneous items such us pride, greed, or controlling others. In the relationship area, the interviewer is looking for mistreatment of the prayee and resulting hurts and wrong attitudes. In other areas, he is looking for participation, for persons who may have induced participation (who thus need to be forgiven), and for ways the prayee has hurt others.

Step 7:   Lead the prayee in "closing" these "doors" to the admission of spirits.

"Leading," in this case, means having the prayee repeat sentences after you, at least in the beginning. After some repetitions, he probably can take the steps on his own.

"Closing a door" involves three or four steps, depending on the situation. Steps B, C, and D below are always included. If another person is involved, step A is also needed.

Step A: Forgive.

The prayee must unequivocally forgive the one who has caused hurt or led him into the wrong conduct, item by item, for each act, each hurtful comment, etc., that the Holy Spirit brings to his mind. After forgiving, he should tell God that he will not try to change the person but will with God's help love that person as he is. Then the prayee should ask God to bless the other person in every way. Releasing and blessing tend to firm up forgiveness.

Sometimes the prayee has been hurt so deeply that he simply cannot forgive the person who hurt him. Explain to him that forgiveness is a decision he makes and is not necessarily a feeling. Explain that if he does not forgive, he will not be forgiven. If he still cannot forgive, ask him if you can pray for him. If he says yes, quietly but firmly bind the spirit of unforgiveness in him and command it to leave him in the name of Jesus. Then see if he can forgive. That may break the logjam. However, if the prayee will not come to the place of forgiveness, you should gently and lovingly bring the ministry to a close. His unforgiveness would just be an open door for expelled demons to return.

The interview and door closing processes can be extremely painful as the prayee relives deep hurts. You may see some or much weeping. You can lovingly stop and ask God to heal his hurts and his broken heart. Do not hurry this prayer. Pray with your eyes open to note any unspoken responses to parts of your prayer.

Step B: Repent and ask forgiveness.

The prayee must repent of his own attitudes, feelings, and acts that are not of God. This repentance includes the conduct itself, such as unforgiveness, resentment, anger, anxiety, pride, taking in rejection, self-pity, or depression. His attitudes and feelings may be very understandable, but if they are not from God, they are from the enemy and should be repented of. Then the prayee should ask God's forgiveness for them. Here too the repentance should be specific, item by item.

Step C: Renounce all sins or spirits involved in the name of Jesus.

The prayee should audibly and firmly renounce his own sin, the effect on him of others' sins, and any bondages. Some examples include the following:

• "In the name of Jesus, I renounce the fear that came upon me when...."
• "In the name of Jesus, I renounce having shared my body with (naming each person) and every unclean sexual spirit I picked up from them. In the name of Jesus, I renounce pornography, fantasy, fornication, and every spirit connected with them."
• "In the name of Jesus, I renounce having put myself under the authority of that (witch, fortune-teller, hypnotist, etc.)."
• "In the name of Jesus, I renounce rejection, loneliness, self-pity, depression, hopelessness, despair, confusion..., etc."

Step D: The minister should break the yoke of bondage and the power of any spirit. Establish eye contact with the prayee and break, in the name of Jesus, the power of the renounced spirits and the yoke of any bondage over the prayee. You could pray like this:

"In Jesus' name I break the yoke of fear, hate, unclean sex, resentment, anger [whatever is involved] *over* [John, Mary] *so that when they are cast out, they will not come back."*

Do not cast out any demons until all "doors" have been closed, or at least all doors in a particular area. If not all doors are closed, expelling spirits is sometimes more difficult, and those that remain when some are expelled may manifest.

Step 8:   When all doors are closed, cast out the unclean spirit or spirits.

Simply cast them out—always in the name of Jesus. It is not necessary to send them somewhere; if the doors have been effectively closed, the spirits will leave quietly and quickly with one or two commands. If they don't, it is a signal that not all doors have been closed. Go back to the interview stage! Find and close the unclosed doors.

The prayee may or may not display some manifestation of the spirit leaving (a sigh, cough, yawn, jerk, etc.). However, he usually will feel free, lighter, like laughing, or deeply peaceful.

When you think you have finished steps 6 through 8, ask the Holy Spirit to show one of you (you, the intercessor, the prayee, and any friend, spouse, or parent who is present) whether there are additional spirits to be exposed and expelled. Wait some moments to see if the Holy Spirit does show someone something. If He does, ask the prayee, gently, whether there is a need in the area that the Holy Spirit has identified. Remember that you might hear incorrectly, so be careful not to speak too strongly and not to be accusatory. If something comes to light, deal with it as per steps 6 through 8.

Step 9:   Lead the prayee in a prayer of praise and thanksgiving to Jesus for his deliverance.

Suggest, as a starter, "Thank You, Jesus, for setting me free!..."

Step 10: Have the prayee ask the Holy Spirit to fill him, to fill up every space formally occupied by an evil spirit. You and your supporters can add similar prayers for him at steps 9 and 10.

If the prayee cannot thank Jesus, if he cannot ask the Holy Spirit to fill him, or if there is further demonic manifestation when he does, it is a signal that there are more doors to be closed and more spirits to be expelled. Ask the Holy Spirit for His help. Go back to step 6 or 7 as indicated.

Concluding the Ministry

Never leave the person receiving ministry unprayed for. General prayers of blessing and encouragement are always in order. But don't overlook praying for his healing—healing of spirit, heart, and body; of relationships; of all emotional needs that have come to light during the ministry. Even if you have prayed for his healing earlier, it is well to do so again. Don't be hurried. Let the Holy Spirit lead you in this prayer time.

Others may want to join in. Unlike the time during the ministry itself, there is no reason for others not to pray, to speak to the prayee, to touch him, or to put their arms around him at this point.

Also, always consider giving him suggestions for staying free. Following are some ideas of the suggestions that you may offer:

- Walking in forgiveness as a lifestyle. Forgive quickly.
- Asking the Lord for healing quickly after being hurt.
- Getting into a support group.
- Getting into a cell group in the person's local church.
- Suggesting ways for changing his habit patterns.
- Taking authority, himself, over any spirits that try to attack or torment him.
- Praying in tongues.
- Daily Bible reading, having quiet time with God.
- Things that you yourself have found helpful in walking in the light.

Discuss these things with the prayee. (Don't overload him!) Consider keeping in touch with him yourself by telephone, letter, or in person, if possible, to see how he is doing and to give him encouragement.

Section IV

Redeeming the Heritage of Power and Purity

Dr. Stephen A. Seamands is the professor of Christian Doctrine at Asbury Theological Seminary in Wilmore, Kentucky. Prior to assuming a teaching position at the seminary in 1983, he pastored United Methodist churches in southern New Jersey for 11 years. "Steve," as he likes to be called, is known for gracefully merging the classical and the practical. His courses on theology and doctrine are taught with a scholar's mind and a pastor's heart. In addition to teaching and working with seminary students, Steve is actively engaged in leading seminars and retreats and conducting renewal events in local churches across the country. He has a particular passion for theological and spiritual renewal within the United Methodist church as well as the larger Body of Christ.

Chapter 10

The Great Divorce: How Power and Purity Got Separated

by Dr. Stephen A. Seamands

In the first two decades of the twentieth century a great divorce occurred among two groups of Evangelical Christians—Holiness and Pentecostal—the effects of which we are still suffering from today. In light of how much they had in common, the divorce between these two groups was entirely unnecessary. It was a feud between members of the same family who at one time looked so much alike that they could have been easily mistaken for twins, and if not identical twins, then at least fraternal ones. But, unfortunately, family feuds are often the most contentious and the most difficult to resolve.

The spark that ignited the controversy and that led to the divorce between the two groups was the outbreak of speaking in tongues at the Azusa Street Revival in 1906. Yet the deeper issue of the conflict revolved around the nature of the baptism of the Holy Spirit, a spiritual experience that both groups strongly believed in. Yet they could not agree as to the nature of that experience: Was the experience primarily about *purity* (cleansing from a heart divided between self and God) or about *power* (anointing for ministry and service)?

In terms of their spiritual ancestry, the contributing authors of this book represent both groups. For example, my spiritual roots are in the

Holiness camp, not in the Pentecostal one. (Both my grandfathers were converted at Holiness camp meetings, and I teach at a seminary founded in 1923 by Henry Clay Morrison, a leader in the Holiness movement.) As a result of our differences and orientations, there will be differences as to how we describe the work of the Spirit in the life of the believer. However, all the authors of this text are agreed that in relation to the nature of the deeper work of the Spirit in the life of the believer, it is not an issue of "either/or" (purity or power) but "*both/and*" (purity and power). We are convinced that the Church has suffered greatly because of a polarizing "either/or" understanding. This has led to a Church too often filled with sanctified people who are without power for ministry and anointed people lacking moral character. Power and purity must march hand in hand. Yet we are also encouraged because there is a current stream of renewal bringing these two groups back together. A wedding—a remarriage, if you will—of purity and power is taking place.

Power and Purity in the Life and Ministry of Jesus

There is no question that power and purity are inseparably wedded together in the Scriptures. If the two sides—Holiness and Pentecostal—had each been able to approach the Bible in an unbiased manner, perhaps the divorce could have been avoided. So before describing how the divorce took place, I would like to consider one example of the many in Scripture where the two are held closely together. This example is found in Luke's Gospel, and it occurred at the beginning of Christ's ministry.

In his account of the baptism of Jesus, Luke, like the other three Gospel writers, is careful to point out that when Jesus was baptized, "...heaven was opened and the Holy Spirit descended on Him in bodily form like a dove..." (Lk. 3:21-22). Of course, this wasn't the first time that the Holy Spirit was active in the life of Jesus. Years before, the angel had told Mary that although she was a virgin, she would give birth to a son because the Holy Spirit would come upon her (see Lk. 1:35). This shows us that Jesus had a relationship with the Holy Spirit from the very beginning of His earthly existence.

But now, on the day of His baptism, as Colin Gunton puts it, Jesus "entered a new form of relationship with the Spirit."[1] Everything in the description—the heavens opening, the dove descending, the audible voice—indicate that something very significant is happening. And since Luke is more concerned than the other Gospel writers to stress Jesus'

---

1.   Colin Gunton, *The Promise of the Trinity* (Edinburgh: T & T Clark, 1991), 37.

relationship to the Holy Spirit, it is important to note the two events in the life of Jesus that immediately follow. Luke is explicit that both are a direct consequence of Jesus' new relationship with the Holy Spirit.

First, Jesus is "led by the Spirit in the desert" (Lk. 4:1) where for 40 days He is tempted by the devil. However, because He is "full of the Holy Spirit" (Lk. 4:1), He withstands the devil's onslaughts and emerges victorious. Like Matthew, Luke describes three specific temptations (see Mt. 4:1-11). When they are analyzed, particularly the temptations to turn stones into bread and to throw Himself down from the temple, it is not difficult to discern the devil's strategy.

Jesus has just heard His Father's words of affirmation, "You are My Son, whom I love; with You I am well pleased" (Lk. 3:22). But instead of calling His identity into question as we might expect, the devil tries to get Jesus to presume on the basis of it: *If You are the Son of God...*" (Lk. 4:3,9). In other words, he was saying, "As the Son of God, You have certain rights and prerogatives, so go ahead and assert them." The devil then doesn't try to stop Jesus from doing God's work. Instead, he tempts Jesus to do God's work in His own way or in the way others want rather than God's way.[2] Jesus, however, through the power of the Spirit, remained steadfast in His commitment to do God's will God's way.

The temptations then revolve around issues related to purity of heart. That which is pure is unmixed and undivided. It consists of one thing and one thing only. As Søren Kierkegaard put it, "Purity of heart is to will one thing."[3] Christ's victory over temptation reveals that He is single-minded and wholehearted—not double-minded and halfhearted—in His determination to do God's will God's way. He is pure in heart. He doesn't want God's will *and* His own will. He wants God's will alone.

Following the temptation, Luke goes on to describe the beginning of Jesus' active ministry. He returns to Galilee "in the power of the Spirit" and begins teaching in the local synagogues (see Lk. 4:14-15). Then in the synagogue of His hometown of Nazareth, He reads from Isaiah 61: "The Spirit of the Lord is on Me, because He has anointed Me to preach good news to the poor. He has sent Me to proclaim freedom for the prisoners and recovery of sight for the blind, to release the oppressed, to

---

2.   According to Oswald Chambers this is also "the central citadel of the devil's attack in the life of the believer." See *The Psychology of Redemption* (Fort Washington, PA: Christian Literature Crusade, 1975), 63.

3.   See Kierkegaard's book by that title, *Purity of Heart Is to Will One Thing* (New York: Harper and Row, 1938).

proclaim the year of the Lord's favor" (Lk. 4:18-19). He then boldly declares, "Today this scripture is fulfilled in your hearing" (Lk. 4:21b). In the days that follow, He heals many who are sick and delivers those who are demonized (see Lk. 4:33-41). As a result the people are "amazed" because He ministers with such "authority and power" (Lk. 4:32,36). News about Him begins to spread throughout the area (see Lk. 4:14,37). Because the Spirit of the Lord is upon Him, He is able to accomplish the mighty works of God.

From this account we may conclude that Luke would have us realize that two things characterize Jesus' new form of relationship with the Holy Spirit. First, He is able to live before God with a pure heart, doing God's will God's way. Second, He is able to accomplish the mighty works of God.

These two characteristics—purity and power—are distinct. In the two events Luke describes—overcoming temptation and initiating ministry—the spotlight is first on one and then on the other. Purity is bound up with *being* or *character*; power with *doing* or *conduct*. Purity has to do with inner motives; power with outer actions. Using Paul's categories, purity is a manifestation of the fruit of the Spirit (see Gal. 5:22-23) while power is a manifestation of the gifts of the Spirit (see 1 Cor. 12).

Yet although these two characteristics are distinct, they are also inseparable. Without power, purity is diminished; without purity, power is distorted. It is significant how Luke reveals the connection at the end of the passage we have been considering.

Because of His power and authority Jesus has "taken Galilee by storm." One evening as the sun is setting in the village of Capernaum, He heals all the sick and demonized persons who are brought to Him (see Lk. 4:40-41). Early the next morning, however, Jesus withdraws to a solitary place to pray.[4] The people come looking for Him. They want Him to heal more people. They also want Him to set up His ministry headquarters in Capernaum. They seem to be excited about what having a healer like Jesus in town will do for the local tourist industry. They have already figured out how they can use Jesus' power to their advantage.

Yet because of His purity of heart, their plan doesn't work. He has been praying, recommitting Himself to do God's work *God's way*, not *His* way or *their* way. So He realizes the threat that His growing popularity poses to His calling. When the people find Him, "they tried to keep Him

---

4.   Luke doesn't actually mention that Jesus prayed, only that Jesus "went out to a solitary place" (Lk. 4:42). According to Mark's account, however, He withdrew to a solitary place "where He prayed" (Mk. 1:35).

from leaving them" (Lk. 4:42). But Jesus is firm in His refusal: "I must preach the good news of the kingdom of God to the other towns also, because that is why I was sent" (Lk. 4:43). Jesus then leaves Capernaum and moves on.

Thus we see in Jesus' life and ministry that the two characteristics that emerge out of His new form of relationship with the Holy Spirit are distinct but inseparable. His purity defines how He will exercise His power. His power is essential in fulfilling His mission, so He will exercise it through acts of healing and deliverance. But because these acts of power can so easily be selfishly misconstrued by others, doing them continually forces Him to continue His focus on issues related to purity.

Purity and Power in the Late Nineteenth Century

It is a big leap from Luke's understanding of Jesus' relationship with the Holy Spirit to the understanding of the baptism of the Holy Spirit that emerged among late nineteenth-century American Evangelicals, particularly among the late nineteenth-century Holiness movement. But we turn there now because it was during this time (especially after 1870) when there was a marked intensification of interest among American Evangelicals upon the role of the Holy Spirit in the life of the believer. Moreover, this period sets the stage for the great divorce that would occur in the first two decades of the twentieth century.

There are a number of excellent scholarly studies that focus on this issue,[5] but one of the best ways to get a feel for what was going on during this time, particularly in relation to American Evangelicalism as a whole, is to read *Powerlines*, edited by Leona Frances Choy.[6] Using a unique interview style based directly on their writings, Choy introduces us to what 24 great Evangelical leaders of this period believed about the Holy Spirit. The leaders include such spiritual giants as E.M. Bounds, F.B. Meyer, Hudson Taylor, Andrew Murray, Samuel Chadwick, R.A. Torrey, Oswald Chambers, A.B. Simpson, Samuel Logan

---

5.   See, for example, Donald W. Dayton, *Theological Roots of Pentecostalism* (Grand Rapids: Zondervan, 1986) and his "The Doctrine of the Baptism of the Holy Spirit: Its Emergence and Significance," *Wesleyan Theological Journal* (Spring, 1978), 114-126. Also see Richard Gilbertson, *The Baptism of the Holy Spirit: The Views of A.B. Simpson and His Contemporaries* (Camp Hill, PA: Christian Publications, 1993), and Vinson Synan, *The Holiness-Pentecostal Tradition* (Grand Rapids: Eerdmans Publishing Co., 1997).

6.   Leona Frances Choy, *Powerlines: What Great Evangelicals Believed About the Holy Spirit, 1850–1930* (Camp Hill, PA: Christian Publications, 1990).

Brengle, Ruth Paxson, G. Campbell Morgan, Dwight L. Moody, and Hannah Whitehall Smith. Although many of these individuals lived through the period of "the great divorce," Choy purposely bases her "interviews" on materials they wrote "before the founding of the Pentecostal denominations at the beginning of the twentieth century" in order to present a clear understanding of "the teachings and experiences of the Holy Spirit *before* that era."[7]

Although they represent various theological traditions, all the leaders included in *Powerlines* agree on one important point. They all believe in the necessity of a deeper experience with the Holy Spirit in the life of a believer *subsequent* to conversion, one where, to use Gunton's phrase again, the believer enters into "a new form of relationship with the Spirit."[8]

The differences among these Christian leaders, however, emerge in two main areas. First, they differ over terminology for the subsequent experience. Some such as Dwight L. Moody, Samuel Chadwick, and R.A. Torrey call it "the baptism of the Holy Spirit." Others such as G. Campbell Morgan, Handley Moule, and Lewis Sperry Chafer prefer "filled with the Spirit," maintaining that one is "baptized in the Spirit" at conversion.

Second, and more importantly for our concern, these leaders differ on matters concerning the nature of the experience. At one end of the spectrum are those like Samuel Logan Brengle and Oswald Chambers[9] who relate it to the experience of sanctification, defining it primarily in terms of cleansing or purity. At the other end of the spectrum are those like Dwight L. Moody, R.A. Torrey, and A.J. Gordon[10] who disconnect it from sanctification and define it exclusively in terms of power for service. In between are the majority who hold to a combination of the two, with some placing greater emphasis on purity of heart and others greater emphasis on power for service.[11]

Of course, much of this interest in the Holy Spirit within American Evangelicalism as a whole was generated by persons within the Holiness movement. Prior to the Civil War, Holiness advocates (most of whom were Methodist) had pressed for a renewed emphasis on the experience that Methodist founder John Wesley called "entire sanctification." Wesley

---

7.   Choy, *Powerlines*, 13.
8.   Gunton, *Promise of the Trinity*, 37.
9.   Choy, *Powerlines*, 32, 68.
10.   Choy, *Powerlines*, 113, 166-69, 294-95.
11.   Choy, *Powerlines*, 191, 214-15, 242-43.

taught that through this "second work of grace" subsequent to conversion, a believer could be "made perfect in love" and be enabled to serve God with a pure, undivided heart. There were those within the original Methodist movement such as John Fletcher who preferred to refer to this experience as being baptized or filled with the Holy Spirit, and upon clarification, Wesley himself did not object to that terminology. But prior to the Civil War, "entire sanctification" was the dominant designation for the experience, and regardless of the terminology used, the experience centered around purity, not power.

Following the Civil War, however, that began to change. As historian Donald Dayton notes, "In the years after the Civil War, the Holiness movement increasingly adopted the Pentecostal formulation of entire sanctification."[12] For example, the report of the sixteenth camp meeting of the National Camp Meeting Association for the Promotion of Holiness (the most important organization in the movement) was entitled *A Modern Pentecost*. It contains a sermon on the "Baptism of the Holy Spirit" by William Boole, who proclaimed that "the baptism of the Holy Ghost is a positive, specific, conscious instantaneous experience" and that Methodism "has taught no other doctrine from the beginning."[13] By the end of the century, Pentecostal language had become dominant within the Holiness movement. There were Pentecostal services, Pentecostal papers, Pentecostal churches, Pentecostal magazines (Henry Clay Morrison, who founded Asbury Theological seminary where I teach, edited *The Pentecostal Herald* for years), Pentecostal denominations (the Nazarene Church was originally called "the Pentecostal Church of the Nazarene"), and even a series of books called the "Pentecostal Holiness Library." All this was a decade *before* the beginning of the movement we know as Pentecostalism.

The shift in terminology also began to affect the way Holiness leaders understood the nature of the subsequent experience. Early Holiness leaders such as Phoebe Palmer related "the baptism of the Holy Spirit" almost exclusively to Wesleyan motifs such as sanctification and perfection. The experience then was about purity, and as to the relationship between purity and power, power was virtually equated with purity. Palmer, for example, maintained that "holiness *is* power" and "purity and power are identical."[14]

---

12.   Dayton, *Theological Roots of Pentecostalism*, 90.
13.   Adam Wallace, ed., *A Modern Pentecost* (Philadelphia: Methodist Home Journal Publishing House, 1873; reprint, Salem, OH: Convention Book Store, H.E. Schmul, 1970), 83.
14.   Quoted in Gilbertson, *The Baptism of the Holy Spirit*, 147.

Later, however, Holiness leaders such as A.M. Hills and H.C. Morrison described the experience in terms of both purity *and* power. Hills, who became the first systematic theologian of the Nazarene Church, published a book in 1897 in which the title summed up his view: *Holiness and Power*. Similarly, in his pamphlet, *The Baptism With the Holy Ghost*, Morrison stressed that this was a baptism that both "purifies believers hearts and empowers them for service."[15] The experience thus had both a negative (purifying) and a positive (empowering) dimension. Even though it was still viewed primarily from the perspective of holiness (purity), there was a growing emphasis on empowering as well. This became the generally accepted understanding in the movement.[16]

The Holiness-Pentecostal Divorce, 1906–1920

As the nineteenth century gave way to the twentieth, a growing number of Holiness people were praying for revival, and there was a growing recognition among Holiness leaders of the need for a "new pentecost." For example, in 1901, George Hughes, a leading member of the National Holiness Association, called for a "world-rocking revival of religion" that would "shake the very foundations of the earth." This revival, "along Pentecostal lines," would provide "a fit opening of the 20th Century."[17]

Five years later in April 1906, under the leadership of William J. Seymour, a poor African-American Holiness preacher, such a revival did break out in a run-down, abandoned Methodist Church building at 312 Azusa Street in Los Angeles, California. But it wasn't the type of revival that most Holiness leaders had in mind. "One of the ironies of church history," observes Vinson Synan, "is that those responsible for new religious movements often become hostile to the results of their work."[18] By and large, such was to be the case this time.

---

15. H.C. Morrison, *The Baptism with the Holy Ghost* (Louisville: Pentecostal Herald, 1900), 31.
16. There was, however, a "third blessing" minority view within the Holiness movement that saw "entire sanctification" and "the baptism of the Holy Spirit" as two separate experiences, one related to purity and the other to power, that were both needed by the believer. Hence one could be "entirely sanctified" but not "baptized in the Spirit"; one could have his heart purified but not be empowered for service. See Dayton, *Theological Roots of Pentecostalism*, 95-100. This would eventually become the official position of several Pentecostal denominations, such as the Pentecostal Holiness Church and the Church of God, Cleveland, Tennessee.
17. Quoted in Synan, *The Holiness-Pentecostal Tradition*, 143-44.
18. Synan, *The Holiness-Pentecostal Tradition*, 143.

Seymour had come under the influence of Charles Fox Parham, who was teaching the doctrine that *glossolalia*, or speaking in tongues, is the initial evidence of being baptized in the Spirit. Parham began to advocate this view after an outbreak of speaking in tongues on January 1, 1900, at his Bible school near Topeka, Kansas. Then he spread the doctrine as he conducted revivals in the Midwest over the next few years. In 1905, when Parham moved his headquarters to Houston, Texas, Seymour spent a few months with him attending classes with about 25 others. Then Seymour felt led to go to Los Angeles.

The revival services at Azusa Street soon attracted national attention, although most of it was less than complimentary. On April 18, 1906, an article on the front page of the *Los Angeles Daily Times* titled "Weird Babel of Tongues" reported:

> "Meetings are held in a tumble-down shack on Azusa Street, near San Pedro Street, and the devotees of the weird doctrine practice the most fanatical rites, preach the wildest theories and work themselves into a state of mad excitement in the particular zeal. Colored people and a sprinkling of whites compose the congregation, and night is hideous in the neighborhood by the howling of the worshippers, who spend hours swaying forth and back in a nerve-wracking attitude of prayer and supplication. They claim to have the 'gift of tongues' and to be able to comprehend the babel."[19]

It must have been a sight to behold! And like most revivals, especially in their initial phases, it had its share of emotionalism and fanaticism.

The Azusa Street Revival continued for the next three years, and it is generally regarded as the beginning of modern Pentecostalism. Visitors came to Azusa Street from all over the United States and Europe. Almost every Pentecostal group in existence today traces its beginnings, directly or indirectly, back to Azusa Street.

Yet, the Azusa Street Revival was rejected by the majority of leaders within the Holiness movement. In December 1906, just eight months after the revival began, Nazarene Church founder Phineas Bresee, who was close to the revival since he lived in Los Angeles, published an editorial that was a harbinger of things to come. Bresee warned his readers to be cautious about anything that strayed from standard Holiness teaching

---

19.   Quoted in D. William Faupel, *The Everlasting Gospel* (Sheffield, England: Sheffield Academic Press, 1996), 190-91.

on the baptism of the Holy Spirit. With its stress on the so-called gift of tongues as the evidence of Spirit baptism, Bresee felt that Azusa Street was causing people to seek "after the hope of exceptional or marvelous things," but "people who have...Christ revealed in the heart by the Holy Spirit, do not hanker after strange fire....There is rest only in the old paths where the Holy Spirit Himself imparts to the soul directly the witness of the cleansing and the indwelling."[20] In analyzing Bresee's response, Holiness scholar Melvin Dieter concludes, "It exhibited a pattern of reaction and judgment which has characterized the viewpoint of the holiness movement in general since that time."[21]

Soon the criticism of Holiness leaders such as Alma White and W.B. Godbey would go much further. In her anti-Pentecostal polemic, *Demons and Tongues*, White, founder of the Pillar of Fire Church, described speaking in tongues as "satanic gibberish" and Pentecostal services as "the climax of demon worship." Following his visit to Azusa Street, Godbey called the leaders there "Satan's preachers, jugglers, necromancers, enchanters, magicians, and all sorts of mendicants."[22] Such extreme and vitriolic reactions would eventually subside. Nevertheless, they were not uncommon during the 20 years following Azusa Street. No doubt they fueled the animosity and widened the chasm between the two groups.

Bresee's editorial, however, reveals the two major ongoing points of contention that Holiness leaders would have with Pentecostalism. The first was doctrinal. They, along with American Evangelicals in general, rejected the Pentecostal insistence that speaking in tongues was *the* initial evidence of Spirit baptism. As Charles Hummel suggests, "This doctrine became the central point of controversy, a 'great divide' between Pentecostals and other Christians."[23] The second was experiential. By encouraging people to seek after sensational, emotionally charged experiences such as speaking in tongues, Holiness people believed that Pentecostals promoted emotionalism and fanaticism. They were afraid that the purity dimension of Spirit baptism would become lost in the process.

---

20. Quoted in Vinson Synan, ed., *Aspects of Pentecostal-Charismatic Origins* (Plainfield, NJ: Logos International, 1975), 74.
21. Melvin Dieter, "Wesleyan-Holiness Aspects of Pentecostal Origins: As Mediated through the Nineteeth-Century Holiness Revival," in *Aspects of Pentecostal-Charismatic Origins*, 73.
22. Synan, *The Holiness-Pentecostal Tradition*, 145-46.
23. Charles Hummel, *Fire in the Fireplace* (Downers Grove, IL: InterVarsity Press, 1978), 59.

Looking back on the divorce 90 years later, it is apparent that these were legitimate concerns. Today most Pentecostals (and Charismatics even more so) have softened in their insistence on tongues as *the* initial evidence. They have also learned to better balance what was seen as emotional and sensational with other aspects of Christian experience.

Yet time also attests to the authenticity of the profound work of God that began at Azusa Street. According to researcher David Barrett, by 1980 the Pentecostals had outgrown all Protestant families of churches. The five largest membership churches in the world today are all Pentecostal in origin.

By their out-and-out rejection of the Azusa Street Revival and the Pentecostal movement, the Holiness people rejected one of the greatest moves of God in all history and missed out on the opportunity to participate in it and contribute to it. And in their ongoing efforts to distance themselves from Pentecostals (and later Charismatics), they have significantly downplayed the power dimension of the fullness of the Spirit, focusing almost exclusively on heart cleansing and purity.

Pentecostals, in turn, also suffered greatly from the divorce. Since many of the early leaders had been active in the Holiness movement, at first they were able to maintain the emphasis on "entire sanctification" as a second crisis experience of purity or heart cleansing, which then prepared the way for a third power experience of baptism in the Holy Spirit evidenced by speaking in tongues. However, as the movement grew and more and more persons from Baptistic and other non-Wesleyan backgrounds joined, the necessity of entire sanctification was increasingly called into question. The issue erupted into a major controversy within early Pentecostalism in 1910 when William Durham preached a sermon at the Chicago Pentecostal convention denouncing the notion of entire sanctification as a second definite work of grace. Because of Christ's finished work of Calvary, he insisted that the believer is perfectly sanctified at conversion and has no need for a later crisis related to sanctification. The later crisis, the baptism of the Holy Ghost, then is solely about power. This "Finished Work" controversy,[24] as it came to be called, raged within Pentecostalism for several years. The result was a major division within the movement with southern Pentecostal groups (such as the Church of God, Pentecostal Holiness Church, and Church of God in Christ) rejecting Durham's notion, and those in the Midwest, North, and West (such as the Assemblies of God) largely accepting it.

---

24.   For an extended discussion of this controversy, see Faupel, *The Everlasting Gospel*, 229-70.

In addition then to its division with the Holiness movement over the relation of purity to power, Pentecostalism was now divided within itself over the issue. The overall effect was to weaken the emphasis on purity within the movement, which arguably weakened the impact of the movement as a whole.

We can be thankful that today there are a growing number of voices on all sides calling for a long-overdue remarriage of purity and power.[25] As Mark Rutland, who has lived and moved in both the Holiness and Pentecostal worlds, puts it,

> "The idiotic cloud of suspicion that hangs in the air whenever holiness and charismatic (or Pentecostal) Christians discuss the work of the Holy Spirit must be dispelled. The Finger of God writes the law of holiness in the heart of the believer. This great work of heart holiness cannot be over-estimated. To lose sight of it is to lose all. However, it must also be remembered that it is by the power of this same Finger of God that Jesus wrought miracles, discerned spirits and cast out devils. A balanced hope of sanctification and a ministry in charismatic power is a holy wedlock indeed. It is a marriage made in heaven, a mirror of Christ, the heartbeat of New Testament Christianity."[26]

Jack Hayford also says it well: "Let us decide now—*to commit ourselves to a supernatural ministry, disciplined by a crucified life.*"[27]

Despite their unfortunate divorce over 90 years ago, it is time, to use Charles Wesley's phrase, to "unite the two so long disjoined"—purity *and* power. And in the current stream of renewal, this seems to be happening. We must embrace a biblical and experiential joining of these concepts in our own lives so that we may realize all that God intends for His children in holiness, power, and life-changing influence upon our world.

---

25. See, for example, Howard Snyder, *The Divided Flame: Wesleyans and the Charismatic Renewal* (Grand Rapids: Zondervan Publishers, 1980); Mark Rutland, *The Finger of God: Reuniting Power and Holiness in the Church* (Wilmore, KY: Bristol Books, 1988); Jack Hayford, *A Passion for Fullness* (Waco, TX: Word Publishing, 1990); Rich Nathan and Ken Wilson, *Empowered Evangelicals: Bringing Together the Best of the Evangelical and Charismatic Worlds* (Ann Arbor, MI: Servant Publications, 1995); Edmund Robb, *The Spirit Who Will Not Be Tamed* (Anderson, IN: Bristol Books, 1997).

26. Rutland, *The Finger of God*, 51.

27. Hayford, *A Passion for Fullness*, 125.

"Nothing motivates me more than seeing the finger of God respond to the hunger, thirst, and desperation of dry and weary followers of Jesus," says Steve Beard. And he wants to see more of it. A writer and speaker about the Christian faith, popular culture, and spiritual renewal, Steve is the editor of Good News, a bimonthly magazine for the United Methodists. His articles have appeared in Charisma, Challenge, Ministries Today, and World magazines. He is also the author of Thunderstruck: John Wesley and the Toronto Blessing. *It is Steve's prayer that Christians in North America "respond to the ravishing and dangerous love of God while that hope may still be found."*

Chapter 11

The Unpredictability
of Encountering a Holy God

by Steve Beard

One of the most remarkable aspects of the current worldwide movement of the Holy Spirit has been a reawakened sense of the awe, mystery, and wonder of God. Within the last several years, events such as the revival in Argentina, the Toronto Blessing, and the Pensacola Outpouring—not to mention numerous lesser-known revival happenings—have caused Christians worldwide to grapple with the controversial phenomena surrounding the work of the Holy Spirit.

Most of us create within our minds a picture and concept of God that fits neatly within a three-volume systematic theology text that we can proudly display on our bookshelves. Somewhere along the very noble path of attempting to explain God and His ways, we tend to domesticate His awesomeness and attempt to create Him in our image. This approach usually works well until God shows up in our midst with His manifest presence. At that point, we quickly discover our faulty misperceptions of God, namely that He is manageable and that His ways are fully rational to humans.

According to the Barna Research Group, a majority of people who attend Christian worship services leave without feeling that they experienced God's presence. Less than one-third of the adults feel as though they truly interacted with God. Stunningly, one-third of the adults who *regularly* attend worship services say that they have *never* experienced God's presence at any time during their life. According to George Barna, "The research shows that while most people attend church services with a desire to connect with God, most of them leave the church disappointed, week after week. Eventually people cease to expect a real encounter with God and simply settle for a pleasant experience."[1]

So what happens when the pleasant experience is replaced with the real encounter? "God is, of course, present everywhere," writes author John White. "But there seems to be times when He is, as it were, more present—or shall we say more intensely present. He seems to draw aside one or two layers of a curtain that protects us from Him, exposing our fragility to the awesome energies of his being."[2] Theologian Guy Chevreau explains: "Theologically, what we are talking about is the omnipresent and eternal God localizing and actualizing His presence, in space and time."[3]

The theological works and journals of men such as Jonathan Edwards and John Wesley have been studied and analyzed within the last five years by curious Christians searching for some way to gain a theological grasp upon the phenomena of falling, crying, trembling, and laughing. Although I had previously assigned these kinds of manifestations to Pentecostal and charismatic Christians, it has been interesting to discover that many of these curious responses to God's presence appeared within my own Methodist and Holiness roots, long before Azusa Street. This often comes as quite a surprise to the heirs of the eighteenth-century Wesleyan revival. Over the decades, our history has been written in such a way as to make it more palatable and acceptable to modern sensibilities. Unfortunately, in the process we have lost sight of the marvelous wonder of God's dynamic presence.

With the Scripture and Church history as our guide, it becomes very evident that when a holy God encounters sinful people, at least one of the following three things usually occur: 1) Sinners are radically converted; 2) Christians are transformed and renewed; or 3) The mind of the saint or sinner is offended and the state of his heart revealed. Just as a storm is produced when high and low fronts converge, so too a storm

---

1. "New research shows people attend church services but do not worship" (Evangelical Press News Service [Minneapolis, MN], September 11, 1998, Vol. 47, No. 37, 3-4).
2. John White, *When the Spirit Comes With Power* (Downers Grove, IL: InterVarsity Press, 1988), 23.
3. Guy Chevreau, *Catch the Fire* (HarperPerenniel, 1994), 45.

of a different kind emerges when the glorious and radiant presence of the Lord comes near.

1.   The Radical Conversion of Sinners

How different would our perception and understanding of God be if we had been one of Saul's companions on the road to Damascus? What would we have done if, as we were traveling with him, a light from heaven suddenly flashed around him and we saw him fall to the ground and then witnessed the following exchange between Saul and God:

"Saul, Saul, why do you persecute Me?" "Who are You, Lord?" Saul asked. "I am Jesus, whom you are persecuting," He replied. "Now get up and go into the city, and you will be told what you must do" (Acts 9:4a-6).

Luke also records regarding this event:

The men traveling with Saul stood there speechless; they heard the sound but did not see anyone. Saul got up from the ground, but when he opened his eyes he could see nothing. So they led him by the hand into Damascus. For three days he was blind, and did not eat or drink anything (Acts 9:7-9).

Without wanting to make this a normative conversion experience, it is safe to say that witnessing the holiness and awesome power in that one encounter would forever shatter your one-dimensional, "Sunday school flannel board" concept of Jesus. Conversion, in this instance, was not merely an intellectual assent to the doctrinal positions of Christianity, nor was it an emotionally cathartic event. It was just plain terrifying!

As one reads the testimonies of early Methodist converts who eventually became preachers, it is not difficult to see a pattern of anguish and terror as they wrestled with Holy Spirit conviction that literally shook their body and soul.

Philip Gatch describes his encounter with the convicting power of the Holy Spirit at his conversion on April 26, 1772.

"Immediately I felt the power of God to affect me, body and soul. I felt like crying aloud. God said, by his Spirit, to my soul, 'My power is present to heal thy soul, if thou wilt but believe.' I instantly submitted to the operation of the Spirit of God, and my poor soul was set at liberty. I felt as if I had got into a new world. I was certainly brought from hell's dark door, and made nigh unto God by the blood of Jesus. I was the first person known to shout in that part of the country. A grateful sense of the mercy and goodness of God to my poor soul overwhelmed me."[4]

Benjamin Abbott began preaching in New Jersey in 1773. He describes his conversion like this: "The word reached my heart in such a manner that it shook every joint in my body; tears flowed in abundance, and I cried out for mercy, of which the people took notice, and many were melted into tears."[5]

Peter Cartwright (1785–1872) attended a meeting in early 1801 where the "power of God was wonderfully displayed" and "Christians shouted aloud for joy." He wrote:

"To this meeting I repaired, a guilty, wretched sinner. On the Saturday evening, I went with weeping multitudes and bowed before the stand and earnestly prayed for mercy. In the midst of a solemn struggle of soul, an impression was made on my mind, as though a voice said to me, 'Thy sins are all forgiven thee.' Divine light flashed all around me, unspeakable joy sprung up in my soul."[6]

Austin Taft was taught that Methodist preachers were "full of wild fire" and that it was very dangerous to hear them preach. Of a prayer meeting in Huron County, Ohio, in 1833, Taft writes, "Eternity with all its dread realities opened up before me and it's impossible for any pen to describe the awful agonies of my mind. It is beyond all human description." Taft continues:

"It seemed to me I had already entered the dark abodes of eternal night, and right here something seemed to whisper to me—that there was mercy for me. I stopped and listened for a moment. What a word—mercy for me. It was the best news I ever heard. From that moment my faith laid hold upon the Savior's promises with an unguiding grasp, and I saw a light in the distance far above my head, which grew brighter as it came near, and when it reached me I fell to the floor as quick as the lightning flash, and that moment was filled with the fullness of God. Old things passed away and all things became new. My

---

4.   Abel Stevens, *The Compendious History of American Methodism* (New York: Carlton & Porter, 1867), 83.

5.   Stevens, *Compendious History*, 86.

6.   *Autobiography of Peter Cartwright* (Nashville, TN: Abingdon, 1856, rpt 1984), 38.

happiness was complete....And I remained motionless for 45 minutes without power to move a muscle. My good Presbyterian father thought I was dead and talked of sending for the doctor."[7]

Although these testimonies may strike some modern observers as highly charged exaggerations, it seems very clear that they were exposed to the terror and joy of a God who shakes mountains and blesses children.

How would our perception of God be different if we were friends of the prophet Isaiah? What would we say to the friend sitting in our living room explaining that he saw

> ...the Lord seated on a throne, high and exalted, and the train of His robe filled the temple. Above Him were seraphs, each with six wings: With two wings they covered their faces, with two they covered their feet, and with two they were flying. And they were calling to one another: "Holy, holy, holy is the Lord Almighty; the whole earth is full of His glory" (Isaiah 6:1-3).

As Isaiah attempts to retell the experience, he tells you that "at the sound of their voices the doorposts and thresholds shook and the temple was filled with smoke" (Is. 6:4). (You can picture the holy terror in his eyes even as he tries to describe the indescribable.) At this point he blurts out with a cry, "Woe to me! I am ruined! For I am a man of unclean lips, and I live among a people of unclean lips, and my eyes have seen the King, the Lord Almighty" (Is. 6:5).

Once again, the explanation for such an encounter is difficult to process. How do we explain Daniel's breathtaking encounter with an angel (see Dan. 10), the glorious radiance on the face of Moses (see Ex. 34:29-35), or the life-giving anointing on Elisha's bones (see 2 Kings 13:21)? Rather than embracing the mystery and sovereignty of the God of the Bible, we often work overtime to domesticate Him so that we can comfortably maintain the illusion that somehow we hold the upper hand in the relationship.

"It is time for Christianity to become a place of terror again," writes Michael Yaconelli in his recent book *Dangerous Wonder*, "a place where God continually has to tell us, 'Fear not'; a place where our relationship with God is not a simple belief or doctrine or theology, but the constant

---

7.   This is taken from a letter dated May 10, 1887, and entitled, "A short sketch of the life and conversion and call to the ministry of Austin Taft." It was brought to my attention by one of Taft's relatives, Margaret Stratton.

awareness of God's terrifying presence in our lives. The nice, non-threatening God needs to be replaced by the God whose very presence smashes our egos into dust, burns our sin into ashes, and strips us naked to reveal the real person within."[8]

Yaconelli points out that religious leaders in the days of Jesus had the same tendency we have today. "The Pharisees wanted Jesus to be the same as they were. His truth should be the same truth that they had spent centuries taming. But truth is unpredictable," he writes. "When Jesus is present, everyone is uncomfortable yet mysteriously glad at the same time. People do not like surprises—even church people—and they don't want to be uncomfortable. They want a nice, tame Jesus."[9]

Over the years, Jesus has been re-formatted into a cross between Ghandi and a sentimental, doe-eyed host of a Saturday morning children's show. We superimpose His image upon our pet political dogmas or water Him down so that our sin does not seem so bad. "How did we end up so comfortable with God?" asks Yaconelli. "How did our awe of God get reduced to a lukewarm appreciation of God? How did God become a pal instead of a heart-stopping presence? How can we think of Jesus without remembering His ground-shaking, thunder-crashing, stormy exit on the cross? Why aren't we continually catching our breath and saying, 'This is no ordinary God!'?"[10]

2.   The Transforming and Renewing of Christians

As the former president of Syracuse University, Daniel Steele was one of the leading theologians for the nineteenth century Holiness movement. On November 17, 1870, he had a powerful experience that shifted his priorities and transformed his life. In describing his baptism in the Holy Spirit, Steele says that he "became conscious of a mysterious power exerting itself upon my sensibilities. My physical sensations, though not of a nervous temperament, in good health, alone, and calm, were indescribable, as if an electric current were passing through my body with painless shocks, melting my whole being with a fiery stream of love. The Son of God stood before my spiritual eye in all his loveliness."

---

8.   Michael Yaconelli, *Dangerous Wonder: The Adventure of Childlike Faith* (Colorado Springs: NavPress, 1998), 110-11.

9.   Yaconelli, *Dangerous Wonder*, 28.

10.   Yaconelli, *Dangerous Wonder*, 111.

Have we experienced the "fiery stream of love" Steele describes? While each of our experiences will differ greatly, there can be no question that all of Heaven longs for us to know and experience divine love.

"I know for the first time I realized 'the unsearchable riches of Christ.' Reputation, friends, family, property, everything disappeared, eclipsed by the brightness of his manifestation," maintains Steele.

> "He seemed to say, 'I have come to stay.' Yet there was no uttered word, no phantasm or image. It was not a trance or vision. The affections were the sphere of this wonderful phenomenon, best described as 'the love of God shed abroad in the heart by the Holy Ghost.' It seemed as if the attraction of Jesus, the loadstone of my soul, was so strong that it would draw the spirit out of the body upward into heaven. How vivid and real was all this to me! I was more certain that God loved me than I was of the existence of the solid earth and of the shining sun. I intuitively apprehended Christ."[11]

In the manifest presence of God, we are given a more accurate understanding of His penetrating and extravagant love. We are given the grace to intuitively apprehend Christ, and our concept of His holiness deepens.

The prolific Methodist evangelist E. Stanley Jones (1884–1973) was one who discovered the palpable presence of God. Before graduating in 1906 from Asbury College in Wilmore, Kentucky, he experienced a remarkable event.

"Four or five of us students were in the room of another student, Jim Ballinger, having a prayer meeting about ten o'clock at night," recalls Jones. "I remember I was almost asleep with my head against the bedclothes where I was kneeling, when we were all swept off our feet by a visitation of the Holy Spirit. We were all filled, flooded by the Spirit." Although none of the students there spoke in tongues, he emphatically states: "Everything that happened to the disciples on the original Pentecost happened to us."

He admits that he was "tempted to tone down what really happened, or to dress it up in garments of respectability by using noncommittal descriptive terms. In either case it would be dishonest and perhaps worse—a betrayal of one of the most sacred and formative gifts

---

11.   S. Olin Garrison, ed., *Forty Witnesses* (New York: Eaton and Mains, 1888), 41-44.

of my life, a gift of God. To some who have looked upon me as an 'intellectual' it will come as a shock. But shock or no shock, here goes."

Being willing to be misunderstood, Jones writes, "For three or four days it could be said of us as was said of those at the original Pentecost. 'They are drunk.' I was drunk with God. I say 'for three or four days,' for time seemed to have lost its significance."[12]

Basking within the glorious presence of God, E. Stanley Jones—who would later become one of Methodism's most cherished cross-cultural missionaries to India—was swept off his feet and became inebriated within the love, peace, and righteousness of a merciful God. What was the fruit of the experience? "I was released from the fear of emotion. I had tasted three days of ecstasy—drunk with God," testifies Jones. "And yet they were the clearest-headed, soberest moments I have ever known. I saw into the heart of reality, and the heart of reality was joy, joy, joy. And the heart of reality was love, love, love."[13]

This life-altering revelation of the love of God draws us into a deeper walk and a more fruitful ministry. Take, for example, the extraordinary example of Phineas F. Bresee (1838–1916), one of the co-founders of the Church of the Nazarene. He describes an unforgettable encounter with a holy God one evening while he was sitting near the opened door of his parsonage.

> "As I waited and waited, and continued in prayer, looking up, it seemed to me as if from the azure there came a meteor, an indescribable ball of condensed light, descending rapidly toward me. As I gazed upon it, it was soon within a few score feet, when I seemed distinctly to hear a voice saying, as my face was upturned towards it: 'Swallow it; swallow it,' and in an instant it fell upon my lips and face. I attempted to obey the injunction. It seemed to me, however, that I swallowed only a little of it, although it felt like fire on my lips, and the burning sensation did not leave them for several days."

Taken as an isolated incident within the life of this holiness preacher, this experience would leave us all with a great deal more questions than answers—something that God seems quite content to do within our lives. Nevertheless, Bresee goes on to explain that there came within the experience "into my heart and being, a transformed condition of life and

---

12.   E. Stanley Jones, *A Song of Ascents: A Spiritual Biography* (Nashville, TN: Abingdon, 1968), 68.

13.   Jones, *Song*, 69.

blessing and unction and glory, which I had never known before. I felt that my need was supplied." Although he admits that he said very little publicly in relation to the encounter,

> "There came into my ministry a new element of spiritual life and power. People began to come into the blessing of full salvation; there were more persons converted; and the last year of my ministry in that church was more consecutively successful, being crowned by an almost constant revival. When the third year came to a close, the church had been nearly doubled in membership, and in every way built up."[14]

Interestingly enough, Henry Clay Morrison (1857–1942), the founder of Asbury Theological Seminary in Wilmore, Kentucky, had a very similar experience. He was outside of Cincinnati, Ohio, with his friend, Dr. Young. After debating whether or not to draw some revival meetings to a close, Morrison felt the presence of God.

"Doctor," said Morrison, "I feel the power of God here in this room right now."

Later he testified: "At that instant the Holy Ghost fell upon me. I fell over on the divan utterly helpless. It seemed as if a great hand had taken hold upon my heart, and was pulling it out of my body. Dr. Young ran across the room, caught me in his arms, and called aloud, but I could not answer."[15]

Morrison says that just "as I came to myself and recovered the use of my limbs, a round ball of liquid fire seemed to strike me in the face, dissolve, and enter into me. I leaped up and shouted aloud, 'Glory to God!' "[16] Dr. Young, who was holding Morrison in his arms, threw him back on to the couch and said, "Morrison, what do you mean? You frightened me fearfully. I thought you were dying."

"Why did you act that way?" asked the doctor. "I did not do anything, Doctor," said Morrison, "the Lord did it."[17] Morrison testifies to being "lifted up so closely in touch with the supernatural that I had but

---

14. E.A. Girvin, *Phineas F. Bresee: A Prince in Israel* (Kansas City, MO: Pentecostal Nazarene Publishing House, 1916), 82-83.

15. H.C. Morrison, *Life Sketches and Sermons* (Louisville, KY: Pentecostal Publishing Company, 1903).

16. Cited in Percival A. Wesche, *Henry Clay Morrison: Crusader Saint* (Wilmore, KY: Asbury Theological Seminary, 1963), 44. Quoted from *The Pentecostal Herald* (Louisville, KY).

17. Wesche, *Henry Clay Morrison*, 44.

little thought of material things. I was floating in what seemed to me a fathomless sea of peace and joy."[18]

Dr. Young was indignant and cautioned him not to become a fanatic. Nevertheless, Morrison's ministry was transformed. He reveals that "under my preaching, while I was under the baptism of the Spirit, there was an almost irresistible power. It was never so at any other time. And if we as preachers would keep so close to God as to be ever under this influence, would not his word truly 'run and be glorified' and a veritable Pentecost be repeated in these later days?"[19]

3.   Offending the Mind to Reveal the Heart

Whenever I hear the call for the return of New Testament Christianity, I am always reminded of the haunting story of Ananias and Sapphira found in Acts 5. This is the story of the husband and wife who sold a piece of property in order to help out the church. In the process, they both lied to the apostles (and to the Holy Spirit, according to Peter) about how much money they were keeping for themselves. When Ananias heard Peter's rebuke, he fell down and died. About three hours later, the same thing happened to his wife, Sapphira. As a result, Scripture says, "Great fear seized the whole church and all who heard about these events" (Acts 5:11).

Now, this is New Testament Christianity. And quite honestly, it is terrifying. The holiness of God is not something to be treated lightly. I recalled the Ananias and Sapphira story as I was reading Abel Steven's *History of American Methodism*, published in 1867. He writes about the persecution that early Methodist preachers faced in Salem, New Jersey, during the Revolutionary War.

> "A profane club of the town continued the persecution, in burlesque imitations of the Methodist worship, but was suddenly arrested by an appalling occurrence in one of their assemblies...While they were amusing themselves with jocular recitations of hymns and exhortations, a female guest rose on a bench to imitate a Methodist class. 'Glory to God!' she exclaimed, 'I have found peace, I am sanctified; I am now ready to die!' At the last word, she fell to the floor a corpse. The club, struck with consternation never assembled again,

---

18.   *Autobiography of Bishop Henry Clay Morrison*, revised and edited by George H. Means (Nashville, TN: Publishing House of the M.E. Church, South, 1917), 31-32.

19.   *Autobiography of Bishop Henry Clay Morrison*, Means, ed., 32.

and Methodism became eminently influential in the town and all its vicinity."[20]

Two hundred pages later, in the chapter dealing with the period of 1796–1804, Stevens recounts another similar incident. This time, Henry Boehm is quoted as reporting on the opposition the Methodists faced in Reading, Pennsylvania. He says that while some men were meeting together,

"...a young man undertook to mimic the Methodists. He went on to show how they acted in their meetings. He shouted, clapped his hands and then he would show how they fell down. (The Methodists in that day would sometimes fall and lose their strength.) He then threw himself down on the floor, and lay there as if asleep. His companions enjoyed the sport; but after he had lain for sometime they wondered why he did not get up. They shook him in order to awake him. When they saw he did not breathe, they turned pale, and sent for a physician, who examined the man, and pronounced him dead. This awful incident did two things for us: it stopped ridicule and persecution; it also gave us favor in the sight of the people. They believed that God was for us."[21]

It goes without saying that these are not exactly the kinds of stories that we want to share with non-believers in order to persuade them to turn to Christ. Nevertheless, this kind of ominous power is part of the package. "The same love that can ravish us can also consume us by its flames," observes John White. "And though the idea of being ravished in the flames of holy love may sound poetic, even romantic, we are not sure whether we want such a dangerous kind of love."[22]

The perilous nature of God's presence in our midst is still true, even if it makes us uncomfortable. "On the whole, I do not find Christians, outside the catacombs, sufficiently sensible of the conditions," observes novelist Annie Dillard. "Does anyone have the foggiest idea what sort of power we so blithely invoke? Or, as I suspect, does no one believe a word of it? The churches are children playing on the floor with their chemistry sets, mixing up a batch of TNT to kill a Sunday morning.

---

20.   Stevens, *Compendious History*, 147.
21.   Stevens, *Compendious History*, 354
22.   John White, *The Pathway of Holiness: A Guide for Sinner* (Downers Grove, IL: Inter-Varsity Press, 1996), 15.

It is madness to wear ladies' straw hats and velvet hats to church; we should all be wearing crash helmets. Ushers should issue life preservers and signal flares; they should lash us to our pews."[23]

There is no telling what Annie Dillard would have thought of the Cane Ridge camp meeting held in Bourbon County, Kentucky. In August of 1801, there were crowds estimated from 10,000 to 25,000 gathered. The Methodist circuit rider Peter Cartwright testifies that he saw "more than a hundred sinners fall like dead men under one powerful sermon, and I have seen and heard more than five hundred Christians all shouting aloud the high praises of God at once; and I will venture to assert that many happy thousands were awakened and converted to God at these camp meetings." What was the response of the onlookers? "Some sinners mocked, some of the old dry professors opposed," recalls Cartwright, "some of the old starched Presbyterian preachers preached against these exercises, but still the work went on and spread almost in every direction, gathering additional force, until our country seemed all coming home to God."[24]

Cartwright reminds us that God will do things however He wants to do them. No matter what the mockers or theologians say or think, God is free to do whatever He wants done. In describing the common revival phenomena of involuntary bodily jerking, Cartwright stated: "I always looked upon the jerks as a judgment sent from God, first, to bring sinners to repentance; and, secondly, to show professors that God would work with or without means, and that he could work over and above means, and do whatsoever seemeth to him good, to the glory of his grace and the salvation of the world."[25]

Marching under the banner of "Blood and Fire," the Salvation Army insisted on going to the least, the last, and the lost. Founded by William and Catherine Booth in the slums of London in 1865, they pursued holiness in their private lives and preached Jesus in the streets. Within Salvation Army history, there emerged a peculiar phenomena known as the "glory fits." During one meeting led by Commissioner Elijah Cadman, "about a hundred persons were in 'glory fits.' " According to Cadman, people came up to the leaders saying, "I don't believe in this," and while speaking these same people "fell under the strange manifestation of the Divine Presence." Cadman explains that the "glory fits" were

---

23.   Annie Dillard, *Teaching a Stone to Talk* (New York: Harper & Row, 1982), 40-41.

24.   *Autobiography of Peter Cartwright*, 43.

25.   *Autobiography of Peter Cartwright*, 46.

"ecstacies during which the individuals affected were insensible, usually silent, and remained thus for one, or many hours....The prostrations were commoner in Holiness services and nights of prayer. Medical and other means devised to control or restrict the symptoms were useless."

Cadman described the experience as

"...nothing but a complete conquering of the body by the soul in its reach upward to its Creator and Redeemer. It is the con- descension of Infinite Love in Christ to so uplift it to Himself for a foretaste of joy with Him in Heaven....We could not say when, where, or how they would occur, and we certainly did not know how God worked—we only saw them as signs of His Presence. People were more curious and bothered about them, of course. That's the way of the human mind. But con- version is much more of a miracle; that is the entire change of a nature and its inclination in a moment, the instantaneous shutting of the door on the power of the Devil and sin, and the opening of blind eyes to the reality of God, His Christ, and Salvation."[26]

Cadman resigned himself to the fact that a sovereign move of God was bursting out in his midst and that it was best to allow the Lord to have His way. He also realized that God was more than willing to offend the mind to reveal the thoughts of the heart.

4.   The Fruit of God's Presence

It is not my intention to make the case for curious revival phenom- ena such as jerking, laughing, trembling, or falling. It is my intent, how- ever, to make clear that there is a certain unpredictability when we encounter the holiness of God. Strange things can and often will occur. Nevertheless, the most important element of the power encounter with God is to produce good fruit in the lives of those whose hearts are stead- fast after Him (see Mt. 7:20).

Within particular seasons throughout John Wesley's entire life, he saw people weeping, violently shaking, crying out, losing consciousness, falling down, and occasionally becoming uncontrollably agitated during his meetings. In response to one who was concerned about the "strange work" that occurred in his meetings, Wesley testifies: "I have seen (as far

---

26.   Humphrey Wallis, *The Happy Warrior: The Life-Story of Commissioner Elijah Cadman* (London: Salvationist Publishing and Supplies, Limited, 1928), 107-12.

as a thing of this kind can be seen) very many persons changed in a moment from the spirit of fear, horror, despair, to the spirit of love, joy, and peace; and from sinful desire, till then reigning over them, to a pure desire of doing the will of God. These are matters of fact, whereof I have been, and almost am, an eye or ear witness."

Wesley continues: "I will show you him that was a lion till then, and is now a lamb; him that was a drunkard, and is now exemplarily sober; the whoremonger that was, who now abhors the very garment spotted by the flesh." Wesley judged by the "whole tenor" of their lives and called these people his "living arguments."

He then offers the following remarkable explanation for the outward signs:

> "Perhaps it might be because of the hardness of our hearts, unready to receive any thing unless we see it with our eyes and hear it with our ears, that God, in tender condescension to our weakness, suffered so many outward signs of the very time when he wrought this inward change to be continually seen and heard among us."[27]

Wesley was 81 years old when he recorded the following episode at one of his meetings: "After preaching to an earnest congregation at Coleford, I met the Society. They contained themselves pretty well during the exhortation, but when I began to pray the flame broke out: many cried aloud; many sunk to the ground; many trembled exceedingly; but all seemed to be quite athirst for God, and penetrated by the presence of his power."[28]

What a scene that must have been in 1784, fully 45 years after the Wesleyan revival began to set England ablaze with the fiery holiness and love of God. Wesley records the phenomenal occurrence almost nonchalantly, as if it was merely one more Methodist meeting.

When Wesley prayed, he says that the flame broke out. That same fire of God's holiness is available to us today. But we must be like the men and women in Wesley's meeting: "athirst for God, and penetrated by the presence of his power."

---

27. John Wesley, *The Works of John Wesley*, 3rd ed., Vol. I, 196 (May 20, 1739).
28. Wesley, Vol. IV, 288 (September 8, 1784).

Other
Destiny Image titles
you will enjoy reading

THE LOST PASSIONS OF JESUS
by Donald L. Milam, Jr.

What motivated Jesus to pursue the cross? What inner strength kept His feet on the path laid before Him? Time and tradition have muted the Church's knowledge of the passions that burned in Jesus' heart, but if we want to—if we dare to—we can still seek those same passions. Learn from a close look at Jesus' own life and words and from the writings of other dedicated followers the passions that enflamed the Son of God and changed the world forever!

ISBN 0-9677402-0-7

THE ASCENDED LIFE
by Bernita J. Conway.

A believer does not need to wait until Heaven to experience an intimate relationship with the Lord. When you are born again, your life becomes His, and He pours His life into yours. Here Bernita Conway explains from personal study and experience the truth of "abiding in the Vine," the Lord Jesus Christ. When you grasp this understanding and begin to walk in it, it will change your whole life and relationship with your heavenly Father!

ISBN 1-56043-337-X

THE MARTYRS' TORCH
by Bruce Porter.

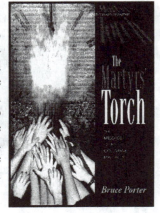

In every age of history, darkness has threatened to extinguish the light. But also in every age of history, heroes and heroines of the faith rose up to hold high the torch of their testimony—witnesses to the truth of the gospel of Jesus Christ. On a fateful spring day at Columbine High, others lifted up their torches and joined the crimson path of the martyrs' way. We cannot forget their sacrifice. A call is sounding forth from Heaven: "Who will take up the martyrs' torch which fell from these faithful hands?" Will you?

ISBN 0-7684-2046-6

Available at your local Christian bookstore.

Internet: http://www.reapernet.com

Other Destiny Image *titles* you will enjoy reading

GOD'S FAVORITE HOUSE

by Tommy Tenney.

The burning desire of your heart can be fulfilled. God is looking for people just like you. He is a Lover in search of a people who will love Him in return. He is far more interested in you than He is interested in a building. He would hush all of Heaven's hosts to listen to your voice raised in heartfelt love songs to Him. This book will show you how to build a house of worship within, fulfilling your heart's desire and His!

ISBN 0-7684-2043-1

THE GOD CHASERS (Best-selling **Destiny Image** book)

by Tommy Tenney.

There are those so hungry, so desperate for His presence, that they become consumed with finding Him. Their longing for Him moves them to do what they would otherwise never do: Chase God. But what does it really mean to chase God? Can He be "caught"? Is there an end to the thirsting of man's soul for Him? Meet Tommy Tenney—God chaser. Join him in his search for God. Follow him as he ignores the maze of religious tradition and finds himself, not chasing God, but to his utter amazement, caught by the One he had chased.

ISBN 0-7684-2016-4

GOD CHASERS DAILY MEDITATION & PERSONAL JOURNAL

by Tommy Tenney.

Does your heart yearn to have an intimate relationship with your Lord? Perhaps you long to draw closer to your heavenly Father, but you don't know how or where to start. This *Daily Meditation & Personal Journal* will help you begin a journey that will change your life. As you read and journal, you'll find your spirit running to meet Him with a desire and fervor you've never before experienced. Let your heart hunger propel you into the chase of your life…after God!

ISBN 0-7684-2040-7

SECRETS OF THE MOST HOLY PLACE

by Don Nori.

Here is a prophetic parable you will read again and again. The winds of God are blowing, drawing you to His Life within the Veil of the Most Holy Place. There you begin to see as you experience a depth of relationship your heart has yearned for. This book is a living, dynamic experience with God!

ISBN 1-56043-076-1

Available at your local Christian bookstore.

Internet: http://www.reapernet.com